A STUDY IN CONSCIOUSNESS

A STUDY IN CONSCIOUSNESS

A CONTRIBUTION TO THE SCIENCE OF PSYCHOLOGY

By
ANNIE BESANT

*Theosophical Society
Centenary Printing*

1975
THE THEOSOPHICAL PUBLISHING HOUSE
ADYAR, MADRAS 600020, INDIA
68, Great Russell Street, London, WCIB 3BU, England
Post Box 270, Wheaton, Illinois 60187, U.S.A.

First Printed	1904
Reprinted	1907
,,	1912
,,	1918
,,	1925
First ADYAR Edition	1938
Second ,, Printing	1947
Third ,, ,,	1954
Fourth ,, ,,	1959
Fifth ,, ,,	1967
Sixth ,, ,,	1972
Seventh ,, ,,	1975

ISBN 0-8356-7287-5 (U.S.A.)

theosophy

PRINTED IN INDIA

At the Vasanta Press, The Theosophical Society,
Adyar, Madras 600020

FOREWORD

THIS book is intended as an aid to students in their study of the growth and development of consciousness, offering hints and suggestions which may prove serviceable to them. It does not pretend to be a complete exposition, but rather, as its sub-title states, a contribution to the science of Psychology. Far ampler materials than are within my reach are necessary for any complete exposition of the far-reaching science which deals with the unfolding of consciousness. These materials are slowly accumulating in the hands of earnest and painstaking students, but no effort has yet been made to arrange and systematise them into a co-ordinated whole. In this little volume I have only arranged a small part of this material, in the hope that it may be useful now to some of the toilers in the great field of the Evolution of Consciousness, and may serve, in the future, as a stone in the complete building. It will need a great architect to plan that temple of knowledge, and skilful master masons to direct the building; enough, for the moment, to do the apprentice task, and prepare the rough stones for the use of more expert workmen.

ANNIE BESANT

CONTENTS

PART I

CONSCIOUSNESS

CONTENTS

PART II

WILL, DESIRE, AND EMOTION

CONTENTS

PART I

CONSCIOUSNESS

INTRODUCTION

THE subject of the unfolding of consciousness in the beings whose field of evolution is a solar system is one of considerable difficulty; none of us may at present hope to do more than master a small portion of its complexity, but it may be possible to study it in such fashion as may fill up some of the gaps in our thinking, and as may yield us a fairly clear outline to guide our future work.

We cannot, however, trace this outline in any way satisfactory to the intelligence, without considering first our solar system as a whole, and endeavouring to grasp some idea, however vague that idea may be, of " the beginnings " in such a system.

1. ORIGINS

We have learned that the matter in a solar system exists in seven great modifications, or planes; on three of these, the physical, emotional (astral) and mental—often spoken of as " the three worlds", the well-known Triloki, or Tribhuvanam, of the Hindu

cosmogony—is proceeding the normal evolution of
humanity. On the next two planes, the spiritual—
those of wisdom and power, the buddhic and the
atmic—goes on the specific evolution of the Initiate,
after the first of the Great Initiations. These five
planes form the field of the evolution of consciousness, until the human merges in the divine. The
two planes beyond the five represent the sphere of
divine activity, encircling and enveloping all, out of
which pour fourth all the divine energies which
vivify and sustain the whole system. They are at
present entirely beyond our knowledge, and the
few hints that have been given regarding them
probably convey as much information as our limited
capacity is able to grasp. We are taught that they
are the planes of divine Consciousness, wherein the
Logos, or the divine Trinity of Logoi, is manifested,
and wherefrom He shines forth as the Creator, the
Preserver, the Dissolver, evolving a universe, maintaining it during its life-period, withdrawing it into
Himself at its ending. We have been given the
names of these two planes: the lower is the Anupadaka, that wherein "no vehicle has yet been
formed",[1] the higher is the Adi, "the first", the
foundation of a universe, its support and the fount
of its life. We have thus the seven planes of a

---

[1] From the *Pranava-vada*, published as *The Science of the Sacred
Word, or The Pranava-vada of Gargyayana.*

universe, a solar system, which, as we see by this brief description, may be regarded as making up three groups: I. The field of Logoic manifestation only; II. The field of super-normal human evolution, that of the Initiate; III. The field of elemental, mineral, vegetable, animal, and normal human evolution. We may tabulate these facts thus:

i. Adi	I. The field of Logoic mani-
ii. Anupadaka	festation only.
iii. Atmic	II. The field of super-normal
iv. Buddhic	human evolution.
v. Mental	III. The field of elemental,
vi. Emotional	mineral, vegetable, animal,
vii. Physical	and normal human evolution.

The two highest planes may be conceived of as existing before the solar system is formed, and we may imagine the highest, the Adi, as consisting of so much of the matter of space—symbolized by points —as the Logos has marked out to form the material basis of the systems He is about to produce. As a workman chooses out the material he is going to shape into his product, so does the Logos choose the material and the place for His universe. Similarly, we may imagine the Anupadaka—symbolized by lines—as consisting of this same matter modified by His individual life, coloured, to use a significant metaphor, by His all-ensouling Consciousness, and

thus differing in some way from the corresponding
plane in another solar system. We are told that
the supreme facts of this preparatory work may be
further imaged forth in symbols; of these we are
given two sets, one of which images the triple manifestation of the Logic Consciousness, the other the
triple change in matter corresponding to the triple
Life—the life and form aspects of the three Logoi.
We may place them side by side, as simultaneous
happenings:

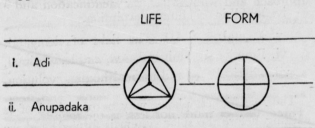

	LIFE	FORM
i. Adi		
ii. Anupadaka		

We have here, under Life, the primeval Point in
the centre of the Circle, the Logos as One within
the self-imposed encircling sphere of subtlest matter,
in which He has enclosed Himself for the purpose
of manifestation, of shining forth from the Darkness.
At once the question arises: Why three Logoi?
Though we touch here on the deepest question of
metaphysics, to expound which even inadequately
requires a volume, we must indicate the answer, to
be wrought out by close thinking. In the analysis

of all that exists, we come to the great generaliza-
tion: " All is separable into ' I ' and ' Not I', the
' Self ' and the ' Not-Self '. Every separate thing
is summed up under one or other of the headings,
Self or Not-Self. There is nothing which cannot
be placed under one of them. Self is Life, Consciousness; Not-Self is Matter, Form." Here, then,
we have a duality. But the Twain are not two
separate things isolated and unrelated; there is a
continual Relation between them, a continual
approach and withdrawal, an identification and a
repudiation; this inter-play shows itself as the ever-
changing universe. Thus we have a Trinity, not
a Duality—the Self, the Not-Self, and the Relation
between them. All is here summed up, all things
and all relations, actual and possible, and hence
Three, neither more nor less, is the foundation of
all universes in their totality, and of each universe
in particular.[1] This fundamental fact imposes on
a Logos a triplicity of manifestation in a solar
system, and hence the One, the Point, going forth
in three directions to the circumference of the Circle
of Matter and returning on itself, manifests a
different aspect at each place of contact with the
Circle—the three fundamental expressions of Consciousness: or Will, Wisdom, and Activity—the

[1] The student should carefully study Bhagavan Das's *The Science
of Peace*, in which the metaphysical questions involved are ex-
pounded with rare acumen and felicity.

divine Triad or Trinity.[1] For the Universal Self, the Pratyag-atma, the "Inner-Self", thinking of the Not-Self, identifies Himself with it, thereby sharing with it His Being; this is the divine Activity, Sat, existence lent to the Non-existent, the Universal Mind. The Self, realizing Himself is Wisdom, Chit, the principle of preservation. The Self, withdrawing Himself from the Not-Self, in His own pure nature, is Bliss, Ananda, free from form. Every Logos of a universe repeats this universal Self-Consciousness: in His Activity, He is the creative Mind, Kriya—corresponding to the universal Sat—the Brahma of the Hindu, the Holy Spirit of the Christian, the Chochmah of the Kabbalist. In His Wisdom, He is the preserving, ordering Reason, Jnana—corresponding to the universal Chit—the Vishnu of the Hindu, the Son of the Christian, the Binah of the Kabbalist. In His Bliss, He is the Dissolver of forms, the Will, Ichchha—corresponding to the universal Ananda— the Shiva of the Hindu, the Father of the Christian, the Kepher of the Kabbalist. Thus appear in

---

[1] " Power, Wisdom, and Love " is another favourite way of expressing this triplicity; but this leaves out Activity, and duplicates Love, unless Love be taken as its equivalent, since Love is essentially active. Wisdom and Love seem to me to be the same aspect of consciousness; that which manifests above as Wisdom, the realization of Unity, manifests in the world of forms as Love, the attractive force which brings about Unity in a world of separated beings.

every universe the three Logoi, the three Beings who create, preserve, and destroy Their universe, each showing forth predominantly in His function in the universe one ruling Aspect, to which the other two are subordinate, though of course ever-present. Hence every manifested God is spoken of as a Trinity. The joining of these three Aspects, or phases of manifestation, at their outer points of contact with the circle, gives the basic Triangle of contact with Matter, which, with the three Triangles made with the lines traced by the Point, thus yields the divine Tetractys, sometimes called the Kosmic Quaternary, the three divine Aspects in contact with Matter, ready to create. These, in their totality, are the Oversoul [1] of the kosmos that is to be.

Under Form we may first glance at the effects of these Aspects as responded to from the side of Matter. These are not, of course, due to the Logos of a system, but are the correspondences in universal Matter with the Aspects of the universal Self. The Aspect of Bliss, or Will, imposes on Matter the quality of Inertia—Tamas, the power of resistance, stability, quietude. The Aspect of Activity gives to Matter its responsiveness to action—Rajas, mobility. The Aspect of Wisdom gives it Rhythm —Satva, vibration, harmony. It is by the aid of

[1] Emerson.

Matter thus prepared that the Aspects of Logic Consciousness can manifest themselves as Beings.

The Logos—not yet a first, since there is yet no second—is seen as a Point irradiating a sphere of Matter, drawn round Him as the field of the future universe flashing with unimaginable splendour, a true Mountain of Light as Manu has it, but Light invisible save on the spiritual planes. This great sphere has been spoken of as primary Substance: it is the Self-conditioned Logos, inseparate at every point with the Matter He has appropriated for His universe, ere He draws Himself a little apart from it in the second manifestation: it is the sphere of Self-conditioning Will, which is to lead to the creative Activity. " I am This", when the " This", the Not-Self, is cognized. The Point, speaking symbolically—in order to make the suggestion of Form as seen from the side of appearances—vibrates between centre and circumference, thus making the Line which marks the drawing apart of Spirit and Matter,[1] rendering cognition possible, and thus generating the Form for the second Aspect, the Being we call the Second Logos, symbolically the Line, or Diameter of the Circle. It is said of this

---

[1] It is well to remember here that this " drawing apart " is in consciousness only: the *idea* of Spirit is separated from the *idea* of matter. In the universe of phenomena, there is no Spirit unconditioned by matter, no smallest particle of matter uninformed by Spirit. All forms are conscious; all consciousnesses have forms.

in mystic phrase: "Thou art my Son; this day have I begotten Thee;"[1] this relation of Father and Son within the unity of the Divine Existence, of the First and Second Logoi, belongs, of course, to the Day of Manifestation, the life-period of a universe. It is this begetting of the Son, this appearance of the Second Logos, the Wisdom, which is marked in the world of Forms by the differentiation, the drawing apart, of Spirit and Matter, the two poles between which is spun the web of a universe; the separation, as it were, of the neutral inactive Electricity—which may symbolize the First Logos—into the dual form of positive and negative—symbolizing the Second—thus making the unmanifest manifest. This separation within the First Logos is vividly imaged for us in the preparation for cell-multiplication that we may study on the physical plane, wherein we see the processes that lead up to the appearance of a dividing wall, whereby the one cell becomes two. For all that happens down here is but the reflection in gross matter of the happenings on higher planes, and we may often find a crutch for our halting imagination in our studies of physical development. "As above, so below." The physical is the reflection of the spiritual.

[1] *Psalms*, ii, 7.

Then the Point, with Line revolving with it, vibrates at right angles to the former vibration, and thus is formed the Cross, still within the Circle, the Cross which thus " proceedeth from the Father and the Son", the symbol of the Third Logos, the Creative Mind, the divine Activity now ready to manifest as Creator. Then He manifests Himself as the Active Cross, or Svastika, the first of the Logoi to manifest outside the two highest planes, through the third stage of the divine unfolding.

		LIFE	FORM
i.	Adi		
ii.	Anupadaka		
iii.	Atmic		

2. ORIGINATION OF MONADS

But before considering the creative Activity of the Third Logos, we must note the origination of the Monads, or Units of Consciousness, for whose evolution in matter the field of a universe is to be prepared. We shall return to their fuller consideration in Chapter II. The Myriads of such Units who are to be developed in that coming universe are generated within the divine Life, as germ-cells in organisms, before the field for their evolution is formed. Of this forthgiving it is written: "THAT willed: I shall multiply and be born;"[1] and the Many arise in the One by that act of Will. Will has its two aspects of attraction and repulsion, of inbreathing and outbreathing, and when the repulsion aspect energizes there is separation, driving apart.

This multiplication within the One by the action of Will marks the place of origin—the First Logos, the undivided Lord, the Eternal Father. These are the sparks of the Supreme Fire, the "divine Fragments",[2] named generally "Monads". A Monad is a fragment of the divine Life, separated off as an individual entity by rarest film of matter, matter so rare that, while it gives a separate form to each, it offers no obstacle to the free inter-communication of a life thus incased with the surrounding similar lives. The life of the Monads is thus of the First Logos, and is therefore of triple aspect, Consciousness existing as Will, Wisdom, and Activity; this life takes form on the plane of divine Manifestation, the second, or Anupadaka, Sons of the Father even as is the Second Logos, but younger Sons with none of

---

[1] *Chhandogyopanishatd*, VI, ii, 3.
[2] *Light on the Path.*

their divine powers capable of acting in matter denser than that of their own planes; while He, with ages of evolution behind Him, stands ready to exercise His divine powers, "the First-born among many brethren".[1] Fitly they dwell on the Anupadaka plane, the roots of their life in the Adi, as yet without vehicles in which they can express themselves, awaiting the day of "manifestation of the Sons of God".[2] There they remain while the Third Logos begins the external work of manifestation, the shaping of the objective universe. He is going to put forth His life into matter, to fashion it into the materials fitted for the building of the vehicles which the Monads need for their evolution. But He will not be merged in His work; for, vast as that work seems to us, to Him it is but a little thing: "Having pervaded this whole universe with a portion of Myself, I remain."[3] That marvellous Individuality is not lost, and only a portion thereof suffices for the life of a kosmos. The Logos, the Oversoul, remains, the God of His Universe.

[1] *Romans*, viii, 29.
[2] *Ibid.*, 19.
[3] *Bhagavad-Gita*, x, 42.

CHAPTER I

THE PREPARATION OF THE FIELD

1. THE FORMATION OF THE ATOM

THE Third Logos, the Universal Mind begins His creative Activity by working on the matter drawn in from the infinite space on every side for the building of our solar system. This matter exists in space in forms incognizable by us, but is apparently already shaped to the needs of vaster systems. For we have been told by H. P. Blavatsky that the atomic sub-planes of our planes make up the first, or lowest, kosmic plane. If we think of the atoms of that kosmic plane as symbolized by a musical note, our atoms, as formed by the Third Logos, may perhaps be symbolized by the overtones in such a note. What seems clear is that they are in close relation to the " atoms of space", correspond with them, but are not, in their present form, identical with them. But the seven types of matter, that become our " atoms", are indicated in the matter drawn from space to form the solar system, and are ultimately reducible again to them. H. P. Blavatsky hints at the repeated sevenfold division into atoms of lower and lower grade, when she writes: " The One Kosmic Atom becomes seven atoms on the plane of matter, and each is transformed into a centre of energy. That same atom becomes seven rays on the plane of spirit . . . separate till the end of the kalpa and yet in close embrace." [1]

Outside the limits of a universe this matter is in a very peculiar state; the three qualities of matter, inertia, mobility, and rhythm,[2] are balanced against each other, and are in a state of equilibrium. They might be thought of as existing as a closed circle, quiescent. In fact, in some ancient books, matter in its totality is described in this state as inertia. It is also spoken of as virgin; it is the celestial Virgin Mary, the ocean of virgin matter, that is to become the Mother by the action of the Third Logos. The beginning of creative Activity is the breaking of that closed circle, throwing the qualities out of stable into unstable equilibrium. Life is motion, and the life of the Solar Logos—His Breath, as it is poetically called—touching this quiescent matter, threw the qualities into a condition of unstable equilibrium, and therefore of continual motion in relation to

[1] *The Secret Doctrine*, i, 696. (London edn. 1928)
[2] Tamas, Rajas, and Satva.

each other. During the life-period of a universe matter is ever in a condition of incessant internal motion. H. P. Blavatsky says: " Fohat hardens and scatters the seven Brothers . . . electrifies into life and separates primordial stuff, or pregenetic matter, into atoms." [1]

The formation of the atom has three stages. First, the fixing of the limit within which the ensouling life—the Life of the Logos in the atom— shall vibrate; this limiting and fixing of the wave-length of the vibration is technically called " the divine measure "; [2] this gives to the atoms of a plane their distinctive peculiarity. Secondly, the Logos marks out, according to this divine measure, the lines which determine the shape of the atom, the fundamental axes of growth, the angular relation of these, which determines the form, being that of the corresponding kosmic atom ; [3] the nearest analogy to these are the axes of crystals. Thirdly, by the measure of the vibration and the angular relation of the axes of growth with each other, the size and form of the surface, which we may call the surface or wall of the atom, is determined. Thus in every atom we have the measure of its ensouling life, its axes of growth, and its enclosing surface or wall.

[1] *The Secret Doctrine*, i, 105.
[2] Tanmatra, the measure of That—" That " being the Divine Spirit.
[3] Collectively, a Tattva.

Of such atoms the Third Logos creates five different kinds, the five different " measures " implying five different vibrations, and each kind forms the basic material of a plane; each plane, however various the objects in it, has its own fundamental type of atom, into which any of its objects may ultimately be reduced.

2. SPIRIT-MATTER

The epithet, spirit-matter, will perhaps be better appreciated if we pause for a moment on the method of the formation of the atoms of the successive planes. For each system the matter of space around it is its Root of Matter, Mulaprakriti, as the Hindus graphically call it. The matter of each system has that surrounding matter for its root, or base, and its own special matter grows out of, is developed from, that. That Logos, the Over-soul, of the system, drawing round Himself the necessary matter from space, ensouls it with His own life, and this life within this subtle matter, this Mulaprakriti, is the Atma, the Self, the Spirit, in every particle. Fohat, the energy of the Logos, says H. P. B., " digs holes in space," and no description could be finer and truer. That whirling energy forms innumerable vortices, each shaped by the divine energy and the axes of growth, and each shelled with the matter of space, Atma in a shell of Mulaprakriti, spirit in a shell of matter, the "atoms" of the Ādi, or highest plane, the first. Some of these remain as "atoms"; others join together and form "molecules"; "molecules" join together and make more complex molecular combinations; and so on till six sub-planes below the atomic are formed. (This by analogy with what may be observed below, since these highest planes are incognizable.) Now comes the forming of the atoms of the second plane. Their measure and axes of growth being fixed as above described by the Third Logos, some of the atoms of the Ādi, or first, plane draw round themselves a shell of the combinations of their own lowest sub-plane; the Spirit *plus its original shell of kosmic matter* (Mula-prakriti), or the atom of the first plane, is the spirit of the second plane, and permeates the new shell, formed out of the lowest-grade combinations of itself. These shells, thus ensouled, are the atoms of the anupadaka, or second, plane. By the ever more complicated aggregations of these the remaining six sub-planes are brought into being. Some of the atoms of the anupadaka plane, in like manner, become clothed with the aggregations of their own lowest sub-plane, and thus become the atmic atoms, the Spirit now being clothed with two shells, inside its atomic wall of aggregations of the lowest

2

subplane of the anupadaka, and the original Spirit, or Life, *plus* its two shells, being called the spirit of the atmic plane, while the wall of its atom is regarded as the matter. This atom, ensheathed once more in the aggregations of the lowest atmic sub-plane, becomes the atom of the buddhic plane, Spirit on the buddhic plane having thus three enclosing films within its atomic shell of lowest atmic aggregations. On the mental plane the Spirit has a fourfold sheath within the atomic wall, on the astral plane a fivefold, and on the physical a sixfold, with the atomic wall in each case in addition. But the Spirit *plus all its sheaths* save the outermost is ever regarded as Spirit, and the outermost sheath only as form or body. It is this involution of Spirit which makes evolution possible and, complicated as the description may sound, the principle is simple and can be easily grasped. Truly, then, may we speak of " spirit-matter " everywhere.

3. THE SUB-PLANES

Now the ultimate atoms of the physical plane are not the " atoms " of the modern chemist; the ultimate atoms are aggregated into successive typical groups, forming " states of matter ", and the chemical atom may be in the fifth, sixth, or seventh of these states, a gas, a liquid, or a solid. Familiar are the gaseous, the liquid, and the solid states of matter, or, as they are often called, the gaseous, liquid, and solid sub-planes; and above the gaseous are four less familiar conditions, the three etheric states of matter or sub-planes, and the true atomic. These true atoms are aggregated into groups, which then act as units, and these groups are called molecules; the atoms in a molecule are held together by magnetic attraction, and the molecules on each sub-plane are arranged geometrically in relation to each other on axes identical with the axes of growth of the atom of the corresponding plane. By these successive aggregations of atoms into molecules, and of simpler into more complex molecules, the sub-planes of each plane are formed under the directive Activity of the Third Logos, until the field of evolution, consisting of five planes, each showing seven sub-planes—the first and second planes being beyond this field—is completed. But it must not be supposed that these seven sub-planes, as formed by the Third Logos, are at all identical with those which are now existing. Taking the physical plane as an illustration, they bear something of the same relation to the present sub-planes as that which the chemist calls proto-hydrogen bears to the chemical element said to be built up out of it. The present conditions were not brought about by the work of the Third Logos only, in whom Activity predominates; the more strongly attractive or cohesive energies of the Second Logos, who is Wisdom and therefore Love, were needed for the further integrations.

	FORM	LIFE						
Adi								
Anupadaka								
Atma (Æther)								
Buddhi (Air)	Atomic sub-planes	Subatomic sub-planes	Superetheric sub-planes	Etheric sub-planes	Gaseous sub-planes	Liquid sub-planes	Solid sub-planes	
Manas (Fire)								
Kama (Water)								
Sthula (Earth)								

It is important to remember that the planes are interpenetrating, and that corresponding sub-planes are directly related to each other, and are not really separated from each other by intervening layers of denser matter. Thus we must not think of the atomic sub-planes as being separated from each other by six sub-planes of generally increasing density, but as being in immediate connection with each other. We may figure this in the above diagram.

It must be understood that this is a diagram, not a picture: *i.e.*, it represents relations, not material facts—the relations existing between the planes by virtue of their intermingling, and not forty-nine separate bricks placed in seven rows, one on the top of another.

Now this relation is a most important one, for it implies that life can pass from plane to plane by the short road of the communicating atomic sub-planes, and need not necessarily circle round through the six molecular sub-planes before it can reach the next atomic sub-plane to continue its descent. As a matter of fact we shall find presently that life-streams from the Monad do follow this atomic road in their descent to the physical plane. If we now consider a physical atom, looking at it as a whole, we see a vortex of life, the life of the Third Logos, whirling with inconceivable rapidity. By the attraction between these whirling vortices, molecules are built up, and the plane with its sub-planes formed. But at the limiting surface of this whirling vortex are the spirillæ, whirling currents, each at right angles to the one within it and the one without it. These whirling currents are made by the life of the Monad, not by the life of the Third Logos, and are not present at the early stage we are considering; they develop one after another into full activity in the course of evolution, normally one in each Round; their rudiments are indeed completed by the fourth Round by the action of the Second Logos, but the life-stream of the Monad circulates in only four of them, the other three being but faintly indicated. The atoms of the higher planes are formed on the same general plan, as regards the Logic central vortex and its enclosing currents, but all details are at present lacking to us. Many of the practices of yoga are directed to bring about the more rapid evolution of the atoms by quickening this spirillæ-vivifying work of the Monad upon it. As these currents of the monadic life are added to the Logic vortex, the note of life grows richer and richer in its quality. We may compare the central vortex to the fundamental note, the whirling encircling currents to the overtones; the addition of each overtone means an added richness to the note. New forces, new beauties, are thus ever added to the sevenfold chord of life.

4. THE FIVE PLANES

The different responses which the matter of the planes will later give under the impulse of consciousness depend on the work of the Third Logos, on the " measure " by which He limits the atom. The atom of each plane has its own measure, as we have seen, and this limits its power of response, its vibratory action, and gives it its specific character. As the eye is so constituted that it is able to respond to vibrations of ether within a certain range, so is each type of atom, by its constitution, able to respond to vibrations within a certain range. One plane is called the plane made of " mind-stuff", because the " measure " of its atoms makes their dominant response that which answers to a certain range of the vibrations, of the Knowledge Aspect of the Logos, as modified by the Creative Activity.[1] Another is called the plane of " desire-stuff", because the " measure " of its atoms makes their dominant response that which answers to a certain range of the vibrations of the Will [2] Aspect of the Logos. Each type of atom has thus its own peculiar power of response, determined by its own measure of vibration. In each atom lie involved numberless possibilities of response to the three aspects of consciousness, and these possibilities within the atom will be brought out of the atom as powers in the course of evolution. But the capacity

[1] Chit working on Kriya, *i.e.*, Wisdom working on Activity yields Manas, Mind.

[2] Ichchha.

of the matter to respond, and the nature of the response, these are determined by the original action of the triple Self on it, and by the measure imposed on the atoms by the Third Logos; He, out of the infinite capacity of His own multitude of vibratory powers, gives a certain portion to the matter of a particular system in a particular cycle of evolution. This capacity is stamped on matter by the Third Logos, and is ever maintained in matter by His life infolded in the atom. Thus is formed the fivefold field of evolution in which consciousness is to develop.

This work of the Third Logos is usually spoken of as the First Life-Wave.

CHAPTER II

CONSCIOUSNESS

1. THE MEANING OF THE WORD

LET us now consider what we mean by consciousness, and see if this consideration will build for us the much longed-for "bridge", which is the despair of modern thought, between consciousness and matter, will span for us the " gulf" alleged to exist for ever between them.

To begin with a definition of terms: consciousness and life are identical, two names for one thing as regarded from within and from without. There is no life without consciousness; there is no consciousness without life. When we vaguely separate them in thought and analyze what we have done, we find that we have called consciousness turned inward by the name of life, and life turned outwards by the name of consciousness. When our attention is fixed on unity we say life; when it is fixed upon multiplicity we say consciousness; and we forget that the multiplicity is due to, is the essence of, matter, the reflecting surface in which the One becomes the Many. When it is said that life is "more or less conscious", it is not the abstraction of life that is thought of, but "a living thing" more or less aware of its surroundings. The more or less awareness depends on the thickness, the density, of the enwrapping veil which makes it a living thing, separate from its fellows. Annihilate in thought that veil, and you annihilate in thought also life, and are in That into which all opposites are resolved, the All.

This leads us to our next point: the existence of consciousness implies a separation into two aspects of the fundamental all-underlying Unity. The modern name of consciousness, "awareness", equally implies this. For you cannot hang up awareness in the void; awareness implies something of which it is aware, a duality at the least. Otherwise it exists not. In the highest abstraction of consciousness, of awareness, this duality is implied; consciousness ceases if the sense of limitation be withdrawn, is dependent on limitation for existence. Awareness is essentially awareness of *limitation*, and only secondarily awareness of *others*. Awareness of others comes into being with what we call Self-consciousness, Self-awareness. This abstract Twain-in-One, consciousness-limitation, spirit-matter, life-form, are ever inseparable, they appear and

disappear together; they exist only in relation to
each other; they resolve into a necessarily unmanifest Unity, the supreme synthesis.

"As above, so below." Again let the "below"
help us; let us look at consciousness as it appears
when considered from the side of form, as we see it
in a universe of conscious things. Electricity manifests only as positive and negative; when these
neutralize each other, electricity vanishes. In all
things electricity exists, neutral, unmanifest; from
all things it can appear, but not as positive only,
or as negative only; always as balancing amounts
of both, over against each other, and these ever
tending to re-enter together into apparent nothingness, which is not nothingness but the source
equally of both.

But if this be so, what becomes of the "gulf"?
What need of the "bridge"? Consciousness and
matter affect each other because they are the two
constituents of one whole, both appearing as they
draw apart, both disappearing as they unite, and
as they draw apart a relation exists ever between
them.[1] There is no such thing as a conscious unit
which does not consist of this inseparate duality, a
magnet with two poles ever in relation to each

---

[1] That relation is magnetic, but of magnetism of the subtlest
kind, called Fohat, or Daiviprakriti, "The Light of the Logos".
It is of Substance, and in it the essence of consciousness and essence
of matter exist, polarized but not drawn apart.

other. We think of a separate something we call consciousness, and ask how it works on another separate something we call matter. There are no such two separate somethings, but only two drawn-apart but inseparate aspects of That which, without both, is unmanifest, which cannot manifest in the one or the other alone, and is equally in both. There are no fronts without backs, no aboves without belows, no outsides without insides, no spirit without matter. They affect each other because inseparable parts of a unity, manifesting as a duality in space and time. The "gulf" appears when we think of a "spirit" wholly immaterial, and a "body" wholly material—*i.e.*, of two things neither of which exists. There is no spirit which is not matter-enveloped; there is no matter which is not spirit-ensouled. The highest separated Self has its film of matter, and though such a Self is called "a spirit" because the consciousness-aspect is so predominant, none the less is it true that it has its vibrating sheath of matter, and that from this sheath all impulses come forth, which affect all other denser material sheaths in succession. To say this is not to materialize consciousness, but only to recognize the fact that the two primary opposites, consciousness and matter, are straitly bound to-gether, are never apart, not even in the highest Being. Matter is limitation, and without limitation consciousness is not. So far from materializing consciousness, it puts it *as a concept* in sharp antithesis to matter, but it recognizes the fact that *in an entity* the one is not found without the other. The densest matter, the physical, has its core of consciousness; the gas, the stone, the metal, is living, conscious, aware. Thus oxygen becomes aware of hydrogen at a certain temperature, and rushes into combination with it.

Let us now look out of consciousness from within, and see the meaning of the phrase: "Matter is limitation." Consciousness is the one Reality, in the fullest sense of that much-used phrase: it follows from this that any reality found anywhere is drawn from consciousness. Hence, everything which is thought, is. That consciousness in which everything is, *everything* literally, "possible" as well as "actual"—*actual* being that which is thought of as existent by a separated consciousness in time and space, and *possible* all that which is not so being thought of at any period in time and any point in space—we call Absolute Consciousness. It is the All, the Eternal, the Infinite, the Changeless. Consciousness, thinking time and space, and of all forms as existing in them in succession and in places, is the Universal Consciousness, the One called by the Hindu the Saguna Brahman—the Eternal with attributes—the Pratyag-atma—the Inner Self; by the Christian, God; by the Parsi, Hormuzd; by the Mussalman, Allah. Consciousness dealing with a definite time, however long or short, with a definite space, however vast or restricted, is individual, that of a concrete Being, a Lord of many universes, or some universes, or a universe, or of any so-called portion of a universe, *his* portion and to him therefore a universe—these terms varying as to extent with the power of the consciousness; so much of the universal thought as a separate consciousness can completely think, *i.e.*, on which he can impose his own reality, can think of as existing like himself, is *his* universe. To each universe, the Being who is its Lord gives a share of his own indefeasible Reality; but is ever himself limited and controlled by the thought of *his* superior, the Lord of the universe in which *he* exists as a form. Thus we, who are human beings existing in a solar system, are surrounded by innumerable forms which are the thought-forms of the Lord of our system, our Ishvara, or Ruler; the " divine measure " and the " axes of growth," thought by the Third Logos, govern the forms of our atoms, and the surface thought of by Him as the limit of the atom and resistant, offers resistance to all similar atoms. Thus we receive our matter, and cannot alter it, save by the employment of methods also made by His thought; only so long as His thought continues

can the atoms, with all composed of them, continue
to exist, since they have no Reality save that given
by His thought. So long as He retains them as
His body by declaring: " I am this; these atoms
are My body; they share My life; " so long they
will impose themselves as real on all the beings in
this solar system, whose consciousness are clothed
in similar garments. When at the end of the Day
of Manifestation He declares: " I am not this;
these atoms are no longer My body; they no longer
share My life; " then shall they vanish as the dream
they are, and only that shall remain which is the
thought-form of the Monarch of a vaster system.

Thus, as Spirits, we are inherently, indefeasibly
divine, with all the splendour and freedom implied
in that word. But we are clothed in matter which
is not ours, which is the thought-forms of the Ruler
of our system—controlled again by the Rulers of
vaster systems in which ours is included—and we
are only slowly learning to master and use it. When
we realize our oneness with our Ruler, then the
matter shall have no longer power over us, and we
shall see it as the unreality it is, dependent on His
will, which then we shall know as also ours. Then
we can " play " with it, as we cannot while it
blinds us with its borrowed Reality.

Looking thus out of consciousness from within, we
see even more plainly than we saw looking at it

from the world of forms, that there is no "gulf", and no need for a "bridge". Consciousness changes, and each change appears in the matter surrounding it as a vibration, because the Logos has thought vibrations of matter as the invariable concomitant of changes in consciousness; and as the matter is but the resultant of consciousness and its attributes are imposed upon it by active thought, any change in the Logoic Consciousness would change the attributes of the matter of the system, and any change in a consciousness derived from Him shows itself in that matter as a change; this change in matter is a vibration, a rhythmical movement within the limits set by Him for the mobility of masses of matter in that relation. "Change in consciousness and vibration of the matter limiting it" is a "pair", imposed by the thought of the Logos on all embodied consciousnesses in His universe. That such a constant relation exists is shown by the fact that a vibration in a material sheath accompanying a change in the ensouling consciousness, and causing a similar vibration in the sheath ensouled by another consciousness, is found to be accompanied by a change in that second consciousness similar to the change in the first.

In matter far subtler than the physical—as mind-stuff—the creative power of consciousness is more readily seen than in the dense material of the physical plane. Matter becomes dense or rare, and changes its combinations and forms, according to the thoughts of a consciousness active therein. While the fundamental atoms—due to the Logic thought—remain unchanged, they can be combined or dissociated at will. Such experiences open the mind to the metaphysical conception of matter, and enable it to realize at once the borrowed reality and the nonentity of matter.

A word of warning may be useful with regard to the often repeated phrases of " Consciousness *in* a body", " Consciousness ensouling a body", and the like. The student is a little apt to figure consciousness as a kind of rarefied gas enclosed in a material receptacle, a kind of bottle. If he will think carefully he will realize that the resistant surface of the body is but a Logic thought-form, and it *is* there because *thought* there. Consciousness appears as conscious entities, because the Logos thinks such separations, thinks the enclosing walls, makes such thought limitations. And these thoughts of the Logos are due to His unity with the Universal Self, and are but a repetition within the area of a partic- ular universe of the Will to multiply.

A careful dwelling in mind on the distinctions above traced between Absolute Consciousness, Uni- versal Consciousness, and Individual Consciousness

3

will prevent the student from asking the question so often heard: Why is there any universe? Why does All-Consciousness limit itself? Why should the Perfect become the imperfect, All-Power become the powerless, God become the mineral, the brute, the man? In this form the question is unanswerable, for it is founded on false premises. The Perfect is the All, the Totality, the Sum of Being. Within its infinity, as above said, is everything contained, every potentiality, as well as actuality, of existence. All that has been, is, will be, can be, ever is in that Fullness, that Eternal. Only Itself knows Itself in its infinite unimaginable wealth of Being. Because it contains all pairs of opposites, and each pair, in affirming itself, to the eye of reason annihilates itself and vanishes, It seems a Void. But endless universes arising in It proclaim It a Plenum. This Perfect never becomes the imperfect; it *becomes* nothing; It *is* all Spirit and Matter, Strength and Weakness, Knowledge and Ignorance, Peace and Strife, Bliss and Pain, Power and Impotence; the innumerable opposites of manifestation merge into each other and vanish in non-manifestation. The All includes manifestation and non-manifestation, the diastole and systole of the Heart which is Being. The one no more requires explanation than the other; the one cannot be without the other. The puzzle arises because men assert separately one of the inseparate pair of opposites—Spirit, Strength, Knowledge, Peace, Bliss, Power—and then ask: " Why should these become their opposites? " *They do not.* No attribute exists without its opposite; a pair only can manifest; every front has a back, spirit and matter arise together; it is not that spirit exists, and then miraculously produces matter to limit and blind itself, but that spirit and matter arise in the Eternal simultaneously as a mode of Its Being, a form of Self-expression of the All, Pratyagatma and Mulaprakriti, expressing in time and space the Timeless and Spaceless.

2. The Monads

We have seen that by the action of the Third Logos a fivefold field has been provided for the development of Units of Consciousness, and that a Unit of Consciousness is a fragment, a portion of the Universal Consciousness, thought into separation as an individual entity veiled in matter, a Unit of the substance of the First Logos, to be sent forth on the second plane as a separate Being. Such Units are called technically Monads. These are the Sons, abiding from everlasting, from the beginning of a creative age, in the Bosom of the Father, who have not yet been " made perfect through sufferings ";[1]

[1] *Hebrews,* ii, 10.

each of them is truly "equal to the Father as touching his Godhead, but inferior to the Father as touching his manhood",[1] and each of them is to go forth into matter in order to render all things subject to himself;[2] he is to be "sown in weakness" that he may be "raised in power";[3] from a static Logos enfolding all divine potentialities, he is to become a dynamic Logos unfolding all divine powers; omniscient, omnipresent, on his own second plane, but unconscious, "senseless", on all the others,[4] he is to veil his glory in matter that blinds him, in order that he may become omniscient, omnipresent, on all planes, able to answer to all divine vibrations in the universe instead of to those on the highest only.

The meaning of this feeble description of a great truth may be glimpsed by the student by a consideration of the facts of embryonic life and birth. When an Ego is reincarnating, he broods over the human mother in whom his future body is a-building, the vehicle he will one day inhabit. That body is slowly built up of the substance of the mother, and the Ego can do little as to its shaping; it is an embryo, unconscious of its future, dimly

---

[1] Athanasian Creed.
[2] *I Corinthians*, xv, 28.
[3] *Ibid.*, 43.
[4] H. P. Blavatsky, *The Key to Theosophy*. See p. 41, for the principle, though applied to a lower stage.

conscious only of the flow of the maternal life, impressed by maternal hopes and fears, thoughts and desires; nothing from the Ego affects it, save a feeble influence coming through the permanent physical atom, and it does not share, because it cannot answer, to the wide-reaching thoughts, the aspiring emotions of the Ego, as expressed by him in his causal body. That embryo, must develop, must gradually assume a human form, must enter on an independent life, separate from that of his mother, must pass through seven years—as men count time—of such independent life, ere the Ego can fully ensoul it. But during that slow evolution, with its infantile helplessness, its childish follies, pleasures and pains, the Ego to whom it belongs is carrying on his own wider, richer, life, and is gradually coming into nearer and nearer touch with this body, in which alone he can work in the physical world, his touch being manifested as the growth of the *brain*-consciousness.

The condition of the Monad in relation to the evolution of his consciousness in a universe resembles that of the Ego in relation to his new physical body. His own world is that of the second, the anupadaka plane, and there he is fully conscious with the all-embracing Self-consciousness of his world, but not at first of selves, among whom he is separate, of " others ". Let us try to see the stages through which he passes. He is first a spark in a flame: " I sense one Flame, O Gurudeva; I see countless undetached sparks shining in it." [1] The Flame is the First Logos, the *undetached* sparks the Monads. His will to manifest is also theirs, for they are the germ-cells in His body, that will presently have a separate life in His coming universe. Moved by this Will, the sparks share the change called " the begetting of the Son ", and pass into the Second Logos and dwell in Him. Then, with the " proceeding " of the Third, there comes to them from Him the " spiritual individuality ", that H. P. Blavatsky speaks of, the dawning separateness. But still there is no sense of " others ", needed to react as the sense of " I ". The three aspects of consciousness, theirs as sharing the Logic life, are still, to use a figure of speech, " turned inwards ", playing on each other, asleep, unaware of a " without ", sharing the all-Self-consciousness. The great Beings, called the Creative Orders,[2] arouse them to " outer " life; Will, Wisdom, Activity awake to awareness of the " without "; a dim sense of " others " arises, so far as " others " may be in a world where all " forms " intermingle and inter-penetrate, and each becomes " an individual Dhyan Chohan, distinct from others ".[3]   At the first stage,

[1] Occult Catechism, *The Secret Doctrine*, Adyar, 6 vol. ed., vol. i, p. 179.
[2] See *The Pedigree of Man*, by Annie Besant, pp. 11, 12.
[3] *The Secret Doctrine*, Adyar, 6 vol. ed., i, p. 208.

spoken of above, when the Monads are, in the fullest sense [1] of the term, undetached, as " germ-cells in His body ", the Will, Wisdom, and Activity in them are latent, not patent. His Will to manifest is also their will, but theirs unconsciously; He, Self-conscious, knows His object and his path; they, not yet Self-conscious, have in them, as parts of His body, the moving energy of His Will, which will presently be their own individual Will to Live, and which impels them into the conditions wherein a separate-Self-conscious, instead of an all-Self-conscious, life is possible. This leads them to the second stage in the life of the Second Logos, and to the Third. Then, comparatively separate, the awakening by the Creative Orders brings with it the dim senses of " others " and of " I", and with this a thrill of longing for a more clearly defined sense of " I " and of " others "; and this is the " individual Will to Live", and this leads them forth into the denser worlds, wherein such sharper definition alone becomes possible.

It is important to understand that the evolution of the individual " I " is a Self-chosen activity. We are here because we Will to Live; " none else compels ". This aspect of consciousness, the Will, is dealt with in later chapters of this book, and here

---

[1] " The fullest sense ", *i.e.*, with no separate individuality; un-detached, in truth, they ever remain above, ever shining in the Flame.

we need only emphasise the fact that the Monads are Self-moved, Self-determined, in their entry into the lower planes of matter, the field of manifestation, the fivefold universe.   To their vehicles in it, they remain as the Ego to his physical body, with their radiant divine life in loftier spheres, but brooding over their lower vehicles and manifesting more and more in them as they become more plastic. H. P. Blavatsky speaks of this, as the " Monad cycling on downwards into matter ".[1]

Everywhere in Nature we see this same striving after fuller manifestation of life, this constant Will to Live.   The seed, buried in the ground, pushes its growing point upwards to the light.   The bud fettered in its sheathing calyx bursts its prison and expands in the sunshine.   The chick within the egg splits its confining shell in twain.   Everywhere life seeks expression, powers press to exercise themselves. See the painter, the sculptor, the poet, with creative genius struggling within him; to create yields the subtlest pleasure, the keenest savour of exquisite delight.   Therein is but another instance of the omnipresent nature of life, whether in the Logos, the genius, or in the ephemeral creature of a day; all joy in the bliss of living, and feel most alive when they multiply themselves by creation.   To feel life expressing itself, flowing forth, expanding, increasing,

[1] *The Secret Doctrine*, 6 Vol, ed., Vol. i,p, 292.

this is at once the result of the Will to Live, and its fruition in the Bliss of living.

Some of the Monads, willing to live through the toils of the fivefold universe, in order to master matter and in turn to create a universe therein, enter into it to become a developed God therein, a Tree of Life, another Fount of Being. The shaping of a universe is the Day of Forth-going; living is becoming; life knows itself by change. Those, who will not to become masters of matter, creators, remain in their static bliss, excluded from the fivefold universe, unconscious of its activities. For it must be remembered that all the seven planes are interpenetrating, and that Consciousness on any plane means the power of answering to the vibrations of that particular plane. Just as a man may be conscious on the physical plane because his physical body is organized to receive and transmit to him its vibrations, but be totally unconscious of the higher planes though their vibrations are playing on him, because he has not yet organized sufficiently his higher bodies to receive and transmit to him their vibrations; so is the Monad, the Unit of Consciousness, able to be conscious on the second plane, but totally unconscious on the lower five.

He will evolve his consciousness on these by taking from each plane some of its matter, veiling himself in this matter and forming it into a sheath by which he can come into contact with that plane, gradually organizing this sheath of matter into a body capable of functioning on its own plane as an expression of himself, receiving vibrations from the plane and transmitting them to him, receiving vibrations from him and transmitting them to the plane. As he veils himself in the matter of each successive plane he shuts away some of his consciousness, that of it which is too subtle for receiving or setting up vibrations in the matter of that plane. He has within him seven typical vibratory powers —each capable of producing an indefinite number of sub-vibrations of its own type—and these are shut off one by one as he endues veil after veil of grosser matter. The powers in consciousness of expressing itself in certain typical ways—using the word power in the mathematical sense, consciousness " to the third", consciousness " to the fourth", etc.—are seen in matter as what we call dimensions. The physical power of consciousness has its expression in " three-dimensional matter", while the astral, mental, and other powers of consciousness need for their expression other dimensions of matter.

Speaking thus of Monads, we may feel as if we were dealing with something far away. Yet is the Monad very near to us, our Self, the very root of our being, the innermost source of our life, the one

Reality. Hidden, unmanifest, wrapt in silence and darkness is our Self, but our consciousness is the limited manifestation of that Self, the manifested God in the kosmos of our bodies, which are His garments. As the Unmanifest is partially manifest in the Logos as Divine Consciousness, and in the universe as the Body of the Logos,[1] so is our unmanifest Self partially manifest in our consciousness, as the Logos of our individual system, and in our body as the kosmos which clothes the consciousness. As above, so below.

This hidden Self it is which is called the Monad, being verily the One. It is this which gives the subtle sense of unity that ever persists in us amid all changes; the sense of identity has here its source, for this is the Eternal in us. The three out-streaming rays which come from the Monad—to be dealt with presently—are his three aspects, or modes of being, or hypostases, reproducing the Logoi of a universe, the Will, Wisdom, and Activity which are the three essential expressions of embodied consciousness, the familar Atma-Buddhi-Manas of the Theosophist.

This consciousness ever works as a unit on the various planes, but shows out its triplicity on each.

---

[1] In the roaring loom of Time I ply,
And weave for God the garment thou seest Him by.
                                    —Goethe.

When we study consciousness working on the mental plane, we see Will appearing as choice, Wisdom as discrimination, Activity as cognition. On the astral plane we see Will appearing as desire, Wisdom as love, Activity as sensation. On the physical plane, Will has for its instruments the motor organs (karmendriyas), Wisdom the cerebral hemispheres, Activity the organs of sense (jnanendriyas).[1]

The full manifestation of these three aspects of consciousness in their highest forms takes place in man in the same order as the manifestation of the triple Logos in the universe. The third aspect, Activity, revealed as the creative mind, as the gatherer of knowledge, is the first to perfect its vehicles, and show forth its full energies. The second aspect, Wisdom, revealed as the Pure and Compassionate Reason, is the second to shine forth, the Krishna, the Buddha, the Christ, in man. The first aspect, Will is the last to reveal itself, the divine Power of the Self, that which in its impregnable fullness is Beautitude, is Peace.

---

[1] This assignment is tentative only. As matter is the feminine side, Sarasvati, belonging to Brahma, seems to indicate the jnanendriyas, and Durga the karmendriyas.

CHAPTER III

THE PEOPLING OF THE FIELD

1. THE COMING FORTH OF THE MONADS

WHEN the fivefold field is ready, when the five planes, each with its seven sub-planes, are completed so far as their primary constitution is concerned, then begins the activity of the Second Logos, the Builder and Preserver of forms. His activity is spoken of as the Second Life-Wave, the pouring out of Wisdom and Love—the Wisdom, the directing force, needed for the organization and evolution of forms, the Love, the attractive force, needed for holding them together as stable though complex wholes. When this great stream of Logic life pours forth into the fivefold field of manifestation, it brings with it into activity the Monads, the Units of Consciousness, ready to begin their work of evolution, to clothe themselves in matter.

Yet the phrase that the Monads go forth is somewhat inaccurate; that they shine forth, send out their rays of life, would be truer. For they remain ever " in the bosom of the Father", while their life-rays stream out into the ocean of matter, and therein appropriate the materials needed for their energising in the universe. The matter must be appropriated, rendered plastic, shaped into fitting vehicles.

H. P. Blavatsky has described their forthshining in graphic allegorical terms, using a symbolism more expressive than literal-meaning words: " The primordial triangle, which—as soon as it has reflected itself in the ' Heavenly Man', the highest of the lower seven—disappears, returning into ' Silence and Darkness '; and the astral paradigmatic man, whose Monad (Atma) is also represented by a triangle, as it has to become a ternary in conscious devachanic interludes." [1] The primordial triangle, or the three-faced Monad of Will, Wisdom, and Activity, " reflects itself" in the " Heavenly Man", as Atma-Buddhi-Manas, and then " returns into Silence and Darkness ". Atma—often spoken of as the Monad of the lower, or astral man—has to become a ternary, a triplefaced unit, by assimilating Buddhi and Manas. The word "reflection" demands an explanation here. Speaking generally, the term reflection is used when a force manifested on a higher plane shows itself again on a lower plane and is conditioned by a grosser kind of matter in that lower manifestation,

[1] *The Secret Doctrine*, vol. v, p. 426.

so that some of the effective energy of the force is
lost and it shows itself in a feebler form. As now
used in a special instance, it means that a stream
of the life of the Monad pours forth, taking as the
vessel to contain it an atom from each of the three
higher planes of the fivefold field—the third, the
fourth, and the fifth—thus producing the " Heavenly
Man", the " Living Ruler, Immortal", the Pilgrim
who is to evolve, for whose evolution the system was
brought into being.

" As the mighty vibrations of the Sun throw
matter into the vibrations we call his rays (which
express his heat, electricity, and other energies), so
does the Monad cause the atomic matter of the
atmic, buddhic, and manasic planes—surrounding
him as the ether of space surrounds the Sun—to
vibrate, and thus makes to himself a Ray, triple
like his own threefold nature. In this he is aided
by Devas from a previous universe who have passed
through a similar experience before; these guide
the vibratory wave from the Will-aspect to the
atmic atom, and the atmic atom, vibrating to the
Will-aspect is called Atma; they guide the vibratory
wave from the Wisdom-aspect to the buddhic atom,
and the buddhic atom, vibrating to the Wisdom-
aspect, is called Buddhi; also they guide the vibratory wave from the Activity-aspect to the manasic
atom, and the manasic atom, vibrating to the

Activity-aspect, is called Manas. Thus Atma-Buddhi-Manas, the Monad in the world of manifestation, is formed, the Ray of the Monad, beyond the fivefold universe. Here is the mystery of the Watcher, the Spectator, the actionless Atma, who abides ever in his triple nature on his own plane, and lives in the world of men by his Ray, which animates his shadows, the fleeting lives on earth. . . . The shadows do the work on the lower planes, and are moved by the Monad through his Image or Ray, at first so feebly that his influence is well-nigh imperceptible, later with ever-increasing power." [1]

Atma-Buddhi-Manas is the Heavenly Man, the Spiritual Man, and he is the expression of the Monad, whose reflected aspect of Will is Atma, whose reflected aspect of Wisdom is Buddhi, whose reflected aspect of Activity is Manas. Hence we may regard the human Atma as the Will-aspect of the Monad, ensouling an akashic atom; the human Buddhi as the Wisdom-aspect of the Monad, ensouling an air (divine flame) atom; the human Manas as the Activity-aspect of the Monad, ensouling a fiery atom. Thus in Atma-Buddhi-Manas, the spiritual Triad, or the Heavenly Man, we have the three aspects, or energies, of the Monad, embodied in atomic matter, and this is the " Spirit "

[1] The *Pedigree of Man*, pp. 25, 27; slightly modified, as in the book the passage refers to the fourth Chain only.

in man, the Jivatma or Life-Self, the separated Self.[1] It is the germinal Spirit, and in its third aspect the " baby Ego ". It is identical in nature with the Monad, *is the Monad*, but is lessened in force and activity by the veils of matter round it. This lessening of power must not blind us to the identity of nature. We must ever remember that the human consciousness is a unit and that, though its manifestations vary, these variations are only due to the predominance of one or other of its aspects and to the relative density of the materials in which an aspect is working. Its manifestations, thus conditioned, vary, but it is itself ever one.

Such part, then, of the consciousness of the Monad as can express itself in a five-fold universe enters at first thus into the higher matter of this universe, embodying itself in an atom of each of the three higher planes; having thus shone forth and appropriated these atoms for his own use, the Monad has begun his work; in his own subtle nature he cannot as yet descend below the anupadaka plane, and he is therefore said to be in " Silence and Darkness ", unmanifest; but he lives and works in and by means of these appropriated atoms, which form the garment of his life on the planes nearest to his own. We may figure this action thus:

---

[1] The term Jivatma is of course equally applicable to the Monad, but is more often applied to its reflection.

4

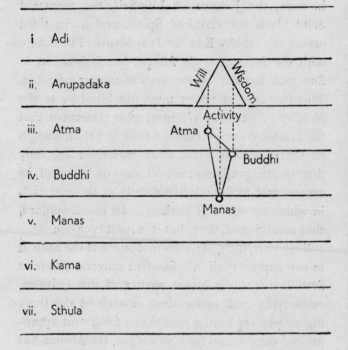

i.	Adi
ii.	Anupadaka
iii.	Atma
iv.	Buddhi
v.	Manas
vi.	Kama
vii.	Sthula

This spiritual Triad, as it is often called, Atma-Buddhi-Manas, the Jivatma, is described as a seed, a germ, of divine Life, containing the potentialities of its own heavenly Father, its Monad, to be unfolded into powers in the course of evolution. This is the " manhood " of the divine Son of the First Logos, animated by the "Godhead", the Monad—a mystery truly, but one which is repeated in many forms around us.

And now the nature, which was free in the subtle matter of his own plane, becomes bound by the denser matter, and his powers of consciousness cannot as yet function in this blinding veil. He is therein as a mere germ, an embryo, powerless, senseless, helpless, while the Monad *on his own plane* is strong, conscious, capable, so far as his internal life is concerned; the one is the Monad in Eternity, the other is the Monad in time and space; the content of the Monad eternal is to become the extent of the Monad temporal and spatial. This at present embryonic life will evolve into a complex being, the expression of the Monad on each plane of the universe. All-powerful internally on his own subtle plane, he is at first powerless, fettered, helpless, when enwrapped externally in denser matter, unable to receive through it, or to give out through it, vibrations. But he will gradually master the matter that at first enslaves him; slowly, surely, he will mould it for Self-expression; he is aided and watched over by the all-sustaining and preserving Second Logos, until he can live in it fully as he lives above, and become in his turn a creative Logos and bring forth out of himself a universe. The power of creating a universe is only gained, according to The Wisdom, by involving within the Self all that is later to be put forth. A Logos does not create out of nothing, but evolves all from

Himself; and from the experiences we are now passing through we are gathering the materials out of which we may build a system in the future.

But this spiritual Triad, this Jivatma, which is the Monad in the fivefold universe, cannot himself commence at once any separate self-directed activity. He cannot gather round himself any aggregations of matter as yet, but can only abide in his atomic vesture. The life of the Second Logos is to him as its mother's womb to the embryo, and within this the building begins. We may, in very truth, regard this stage of evolution, in which the Logos shapes, nourishes, and develops the germinating life, as being, for the Heavenly Man, or truly the Heavenly Embryo, a period corresponding to the ante-natal life of a human being, during which he is slowly obtaining a body, which is nourished meanwhile by the life-currents of the mother and formed out of her substance. Thus also with the Jivatma, enclosing the life of the Monad; he must await the building of his body on the lower planes, and he cannot emerge from this ante-natal life and be " born", until there is a body builded on the lower planes. The " birth " takes place at the formation of the causal body, when the Heavenly Man is manifested as an infant Ego, a true individuality, dwelling in a body on the physical plane. A little careful thought will show how close is the analogy

between the evolution of the Pilgrim and that of
each successive rebirth; in the latter case the
Jivatma awaits the formation of the physical body
which is building as his habitation; in the former
the spiritual Triads, as a Collectivity, await the
building of the systematic Quaternary. Until the
vehicle on the lowest plane is ready, all is a preparation for evolution, rather than evolution itself—
it is often termed involution. The evolution of
the consciousness must begin by contacts received
by its *outermost* vehicle; that is, it must begin on
the physical plane. It can only become aware of
an outside by impacts on its own outside; until then
it dreams within itself, as the faint inner thrillings
ever outwelling from the Monad cause slight out-
ward-tending pressures in the Jivatma, like a spring
of water beneath the earth, seeking an outlet.

2. The Weaving

Meanwhile the preparation for the awakening,
the giving of qualities to matter, that which may be
likened to the formation of the tissues of the future
body, is done by the life-power of the Second Logos
—the Second Life-Wave, rolling through plane
after plane, imparting its own qualities to that
sevenfold proto-matter. The life-wave, as said
above, carries the Jivatmas with it as far as the

atomic sub-plane of the fifth plane, the plane of
Fire, of individualized creative power, of mind.
Here they each have already an atom, the manasic,
or mental veil of the Monad, the Logos flooding
these and the remaining atoms of the plane with
His life. All these atoms, forming the whole atomic
sub-plane, whether free or attached to Jivatmas,
may rightly be termed Monadic Essence; but as in
the course of evolution, presently to be explained,
differences arise between the attached and the
non-attached atoms, the term Monadic Essence is
usually employed for the non-attached, while the
attached are called, for reasons which will appear,
" permanent atoms ". We may define Monadic
Essence then as atomic matter ensouled by the life
of the Second Logos. It is His clothing for the
vivifying and holding together of forms; He is clad
in atomic matter. His own life as Logos, separate
from the life of Atma-Buddhi-Manas in the man,
separate from any lives on the plane—though He
supports, permeates, and includes them all—is
clothed only in atomic matter, and it is this which
is connoted by the term of Monadic Essence. The
matter of that plane, already by the nature of its
atoms [1] capable of responding by vibrations to
active thought-changes, is thrown by the Second
Life-Wave into combinations fit to express thoughts

---

[1] By the Tanmatras, the divine Measures.

—abstract thoughts in the subtler matter, concrete thoughts in the coarser. The combinations of the second and third higher sub-planes constitute the First Elemental Kingdom; the combinations on the four lower sub-planes constitute the Second Elemental Kingdom. Matter held in such combinations is called Elemental Essence, and is susceptible of being shaped into thought-forms. The student must not confuse this with Monadic Essence; one is atomic, the other molecular, in constitution.

The Second Life-Wave then rolls on into the sixth plane, the plane of Water, of individualized sensation, of desire. The before-mentioned Devas link the Jivatma-attached, or permanent, units of the fifth plane to a corresponding number of atoms on the sixth plane, and the Second Logos floods these and the remaining atoms with His own life— these atoms thus becoming Monadic Essence as explained above. The life-wave passes onwards, forming on each sub-plane the combinations fit to express sensations. These combinations constitute the Third Elemental Kingdom, and the matter held in such combination is called Elemental Essence, as before, and on this sixth plane is susceptible of being shaped into desire-forms.

Elemental Essence is thus seen to consist of aggregations of matter on each of the six non-atomic sub-planes of the mental and desire planes, aggregations which do not themselves serve as forms for any entity to inhabit, but as the materials out of which such forms may be built.

The life wave then rolls on into the seventh plane, the plane of Earth, of individualized activities, of actions. As before the Jivatma-attached, or permanent, atoms of the sixth plane are linked to a corresponding number on the seventh plane, and the Second Logos floods these and the remaining atoms with His own life—all these atoms thus becoming Monadic Essence. The life-wave again passes onwards, forming on each sub-plane combinations fitted to constitute physical bodies, the future chemical elements, as they are called on the three lower sub-planes.

Looking at this work of the Second Life-Wave as a whole, we see that its downward sweep is concerned with what may fairly be called the making of primary tissues, out of which hereafter subtle and dense bodies are to be formed. Well has it been called in some ancient scriptures a " weaving ", for such it literally is. The materials prepared by the Third Logos are woven by the Second Logos into threads and into clothes of which future garments— the subtle and dense bodies—will be made. As a man may take separate threads of flax, cotton, silk —themselves combinations of a simpler kind—and weave these into linens, into cotton or silk cloth, these cloths in turn to be shaped into garments by cutting and stitching, so does the Second Logos weave the matter-threads, weave these again into tissues, and then shape them into forms. He is the Eternal Weaver, while we might think of the Third Logos as the Eternal Chemist. The latter works in nature as in a laboratory, the former as in a manufactory. These similes, materialistic as they are, are not to be despised, for they are crutches to aid our limping attempts to understand.

This " weaving " gives to matter its characteristics, as the characteristics of the thread differ from those of the raw materials, as the characteristics of the cloth differ from those of the threads. The Logos weaves the two kinds of cloth of manasic matter, of mind-stuff, and out of these will be made later the causal and the mental bodies. He weaves the cloth of astral matter, of desire-stuff, and out of this will be made later the desire body. This is to say, that the combinations of matter formed and held together by the Second Life-Wave have the characteristics which will act on the Monad when he comes into touch with others, and will enable him to act on them. So will he be able to receive all kinds of vibrations, mental, sensory, etc. The characteristics depend on the nature of the aggregations. There are seven great types, fixed by the nature of the atom, and within these innumerable sub-types. All this goes to the making of the materials of the mechanism of consciousness, which will be conditioned by all these textures, colourings, densities.

In this downward sweep of the life-wave through the fifth, sixth, and seventh planes, downward till the densest matter is reached, and the wave turns at that point to begin its sweep upwards, we must think, then, of its work as that of forming combinations which show qualities, and so we sometimes speak of this work as the giving of qualities. In the upward sweep we shall find that bodies are built out of the matter thus prepared. But before we study the shaping of these, we must consider the sevenfold division of this life-wave in its descent, and the coming forth of the "Shining Ones", the "Devas", the "Angels", the "Elementals", that belongs also to this downward sweep. These are the "Minor Gods" of whom Plato speaks, from whom man derives his perishable bodies.

3.   THE SEVEN STREAMS

The question is constantly asked: Why this continual play by Theosophists upon the number seven? We speak of it as the "root-number of our system", and there is one obvious reason why this number should play an active part in the grouping of things, since we are concerned with the triplicities previously mentioned and explained. A triad naturally produces a septenate by its own internal relations, since its three factors can group themselves in seven ways and no more. We have spoken of matter, outside the limits of a universe, as having the three qualities of matter—inertia, mobility, and rhythm—in a state of equilibrium. When the life of the Logos causes motion, we have at once the possibility of seven groups, for in any given atom, or group of atoms, one or other of these qualities may be more strongly energized than the others, and thus a predominant quality will be shown forth. We may thus have three groups, in one of which inertia will predominate, in another mobility, in a third rhythm. Each of these, again, subdivides, according to the predominance in it of one or other of the remaining two qualities: thus in one of the two inertia groups, mobility may predominate over rhythm, and in the other rhythm over mobility, and so with the other two groups of mobility and rhythm. Hence arise the well-known types, classified according to the predominant quality, usually designated by their Samskrit terms, satvic, rajasic, and tamasic, rhythmical, mobile, and inert, and we have satvic, rajasic, and tamasic foods, animals, men, etc. And we obtain seven groups in all: six sub-divisions of the three, and a seventh in which the three qualities are equally active. (The varieties of type are simply intended to mark in each triad the relative energies of the qualities.)

	INERTIA	MOBILITY	RHYTHM
INERTIA	*Mobility*	Rhythm	
INERTIA	Mobility	*Rhythm*	
MOBILITY	*Rhythm*	Inertia	
MOBILITY	Rhythm	*Inertia*	
RHYTHM	*Inertia*	Mobility	
RHYTHM	Inertia	*Mobility*	

The Life of the Logos, which is to flow into this matter, itself manifests in seven streams, or rays.

These arise similarly out of the three Aspects of Consciousness present in Him, as in all consciousnesses, since all are manifestations of the Universal Self. These are Bliss, or Ichchha, Will; Cognition, or Jnanam, Wisdom; Existence, or Kriya, Activity. So we have the seven streams, or rays of Logic life:

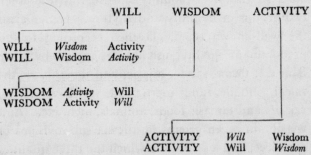

	WILL	WISDOM	ACTIVITY
WILL	*Wisdom*	Activity	
WILL	Wisdom	*Activity*	
WISDOM	*Activity*	Will	
WISDOM	Activity	*Will*	
ACTIVITY	*Will*	Wisdom	
ACTIVITY	Will	*Wisdom*	

All things may be regarded as grouped under these seven headings, the seven streams of Logic life composing the Second Life-Wave and we may think of it as flowing through the planes, descending through them; so that, if we draw the planes horizontally, the life-wave would sweep vertically downwards through them. Moreover, in each stream there will be seven primary sub-divisions, according to the type of matter concerned, and within these secondary sub-divisions, according to the proportions of the qualities within each type, and so on and on in innumerable variations. Into these we need not enter. It is enough to notice the seven types of matter and the seven types of consciousnesses. The seven streams of Logic life show out as the seven types of consciousness, and within each of these the seven types of matter-combinations are found. There are to be seen seven distinct types in each of the three Elemental Kingdoms and on the physical plane. Mme. Blavatsky, in *The Secret Doctrine*, dealing with man, quotes from the stanzas of the *Book of Dzyan*, the fact that there were: " Seven of Them [Creators] each on His lot ", forming the seven types of men, and these sub-divided: " Seven times seven shadows of future men were born." [1] Here is the root of the differing temperaments of men.

[1] *Loc. cit.*, Adyar 6 Vol. Ed., III, 99.

4. THE SHINING ONES

We have now to consider another result of the downward-sweeping life-wave. We have seen that it gives qualities to aggregations of matter on the fifth and sixth planes, and that we have in the First Elemental Kingdom materials ready to clothe abstract thoughts; in the Second Elemental Kingdom materials ready to clothe concrete thoughts; in the Third Elemental Kingdom materials ready to clothe desires. But in addition to impacting qualities to aggregations of matter, the Second Logos gives forth, during this stage of His descent, evolved beings, at various stages of development, who form the normal and typical inhabitants of these three kingdoms. These beings have been brought over by the Logos from a preceding evolution, and are sent forth from the treasure-house of His life, to inhabit the plane for which their development fits them, and to co-operate with Him, and later with man, in the working out of His scheme of evolution. They have received various names in the various religions, but all religions recognize the fact of their existence and of their work. The Samskrit name Devas—the Shining Ones—is the most general, and aptly describes the most marked characteristic of their appearance, a brilliant luminous radiance.[1]

[1] The translation of this descriptive term as " God " has led to much misapprehension of Eastern thought. The " thirty-three

The Hebrew, Christian, and Muhammadan religions call them Archangels and Angels. The Theosophist—to avoid sectarian connotations—names them, after their habitat, Elementals; and this title has the further advantage that it reminds the student of their connection with the five " Elements " of the ancient world: Æther, Air, Fire, Water, and Earth. For there are similar beings of a higher type on the atmic and buddhic planes, as well as the Fire and Water Elementals of the mental and desire planes, and the Ethereal Elementals of the physical. These beings have bodies formed out of the elemental essence of the kingdom to which they belong, flashing many-hued bodies, changing form at the will of the indwelling entity. They form a vast host, ever actively at work, labouring at the elemental essence to improve its quality, taking it to form their own bodies, throwing it off and taking other portions of it, to render it more responsive; they are also constantly busied in the shaping of forms, in aiding human Egos on the way to reincarnation in building their new bodies, bringing materials of the needed kind and helping in its arrangements. The less advanced the Ego the greater the directive work of the Deva; with animals they do almost all the work, and

crores of Gods" are not Gods in the Western sense of the term, which is the equivalent of the Universal Self, and secondarily of the Logoi, but are Devas, Shining Ones.

practically all with vegetables and minerals. They are the active agents in the work of the Logos, carrying out all the details of His world-plan, and aiding the countless evolving lives to find the materials they need for their clothing. All antiquity recognised the indispensable work they do in the worlds, and China, Egypt, India, Persia, Greece, Rome, tell the same story. The belief in the higher of them is not only found in all religions, but memories of those of the desire and of the ethereal physical plane linger on in folk-lore, in stories of "Nature-spirits", "Fairies", "Gnomes", "Trolls", and under many other names, memories of days when men were less deeply enwrapped in material interests, and more sensitive to the influences that played upon them from the subtler worlds. This concentration on material interests, necessary for evolution, has shut out the working of the Elementals from human waking consciousness; but this does not, of course, stop their working, though often rendering it less effective on the physical plane.

At the stage we are considering, however, all this work, except that of the improvement of the elemental essence, lay in the far future, but the Shining Ones laboured diligently at that improvement.

There was thus a vast work of preparation accomplished before anything in the way of physical forms, such as we should recognize, could appear;

a vast labour at the Form side of things before embodied consciousness, save that of the Logos and His Shining Ones, could do anything at all. That which was to be human consciousness at this point was a seed, sown on the higher planes, unconscious of all without it. Under the impelling warmth of the Logic life, it sends out a tiny rootlet downwards, which pushes its ways into the lower planes, blindly, unconsciously, and this rootlet must form our next object of study.

CHAPTER IV

THE PERMANENT ATOM

1. THE ATTACHING OF THE ATOMS

LET us consider the spiritual Triad, the tri-atomic Atma-Buddhi-Manas, the Jivatma, the seed of consciousness, within which the warmth of the stream of Logic life, which surrounds it, is causing faint thrillings of responsive life. These are internal thrillings, preparatory to external activities. After long preparation, a tiny thread, like a minute rootlet, appears, proceeding from the tri-atomic molecule ensheathing consciousness, a golden-coloured thread of life sheathed in buddhic matter; countless such threads appear from the countless Jivatmas, waving vaguely at first in the seven great streams of life, and then becoming anchored—if the expression may be permitted—by attachment to a single molecule or unit, on the fourth mental sub-plane. This anchoring—like the previous one to the three higher atoms, and like the later ones to the astral and physical atoms—is brought about by the action of the Shining Ones. Round this attached unit gather temporary aggregations of elemental essence of the Second Kingdom, scattering and re-gathering, over and over again, ever with the attached unit as centre. This stable centre, serving for an endless succession of changing complex forms, is gradually awakened by the vibrations of these forms into faint responses, these again thrilling feebly upwards to the seed of Consciousness and producing therein vaguest internal movements. It cannot be said that each centre has always round it a form of its own; for one aggregation of ele-mental essence may have several, or very many, of these centres within it, or, again, may have only one, or none. Thus with inconceivable slowness these attached units become possessors of certain qualities; that is, acquire the power of vibrating in certain ways, which are connected with thinking and will hereafter make thoughts possible. The Shining Ones of the Second Elemental Kingdom work upon them also, directing upon them the vibrations to which they gradually begin to respond, and surrounding them with the elemental essence thrown off from their own bodies.[1] Moreover, each of the seven typical groups is separated from the others by a delicate wall of monadic essence (atomic matter ensouled by the life of the Second Logos), the beginning of the wall of the future Group-Soul.

[1] See *Evolution of Life and Form*, by Annie Besant, pp. 132, 133.

This whole process is repeated when the Third Elemental Kingdom has been formed. The tiny thread of buddhic ensheathed life, with its attached mental unit, now pushes outwards to the desire-plane and attaches itself to a single astral atom, adding this to itself as its stable centre on the desire-plane. Round this now gather temporary aggregations of elemental essence of the Third Kingdom, scattering and regathering as before. Similar results follow, as the countless succession of forms ensheathes this stable centre, awaking it to similarly faint responses, which in their turn thrill feebly upwards to the seed of Consciousness, producing therein, once more, vaguest internal movements. Thus, again, these attached atoms become slowly possessed of certain qualities; that is, acquire the power of vibrating in certain ways, which are connected with sensation and will hereafter make sensations possible. Here also the Shining Ones of the Third Elemental Kingdom co-operate in the work, using their more highly developed powers of vibration to produce sympathetically in these undeveloped atoms the power of response, and, as before, giving them of their own substance. The separating wall of each of the seven groups acquires a second layer, formed of the monadic essence of the desire-plane, thus approaching a stage nearer to the wall of the future Group-Soul.

Once more is the process repeated when the great wave has travelled onwards into the physical plane. The tiny thread of buddhic-ensheathed life, with its attached mental and desire units, pushes outwards once more and annexes a physical atom, adding this to itself as its stable centre on the physical plane. Round this gather ethereal molecules, but the heavier physical matter is more coherent than the subtler matter of the higher planes, and a much longer term of life may be observed. Then —as are formed the ethereal types of the proto-metals, and later proto-metals, metals, non-metallic elements, and minerals—the Shining Ones of the Ethereal Physical Kingdom submerge these attached atoms in their sheaths of ether into the one of the seven ethereal types to which they respectively belong, and they begin their long physical evolution. Before we can follow this further we must consider Group-Souls, which on the atomic sub-plane receive their third enveloping layer. But it will be well to pause for a while on the nature and the function of these permanent atoms, the tri-units, or triads, which are as a reflection on the lower planes of the spiritual Triads on the higher, and each of which is attached to a spiritual Triad, its Jivatma. Each triad consists of a physical atom, an astral atom, and a mental unit, permanently attached by a thread of buddhic matter to a spiritual Triad. The thread has sometimes been called the Sutratma, the Thread-Self, because the permanent particles are threaded on it as " beads on a string ".[1]

We may again resort to a diagram, showing the relation.

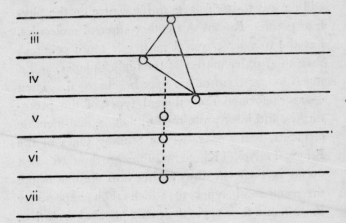

2. THE WEB OF LIFE

It has been said that the connection with the spiritual Triad is through buddhic matter, and this is indicated in the diagram by the dotted line which connects the atoms coming down from the line in

[1] This term is used to denote various things, but always in the same sense, as the thread connecting separate particles. It is applied to the reincarnating Ego, as the thread on which many separate lives are strung; to the Second Logos, as the Thread on which the beings in His universe are strung; and so on. It denotes a function, rather than a special entity or class of entities.

the buddhic plane, and not from the manasic atom. It is of buddhic matter that is spun the marvellous web of life which supports and vivifies all our bodies. If the bodies be looked at with buddhic vision they all disappear, and in their places is seen a shimmering golden web of inconceivable fineness and delicate beauty, a tracery of all their parts, in a network with minute meshes. This is formed of buddhic matter, and within these meshes the coarser atoms are built together. Closer inspection shows that the whole network is formed of a single thread, which is a prolongation of the Sutratma. During the ante-natal life of the babe, this thread grows out from the permanent physical atom and branches out in every direction, the growth continuing until the physical body is full grown; during physical life the prana, the life-breath, plays ever along it, following all its branches and meshes; at death it is withdrawn, leaving the particles of the body to scatter; it may be watched, slowly disentangling itself from the dense physical matter, the life-breath accompanying it, and drawing itself together in the heart round the permanent atom; as it withdraws, the deserted limbs grow cold—its absence makes the " death-chill"; the golden-violet flame of the life-breath is seen shining around it in the heart, and the flame, and the golden life-web, and the permanent atom rise along the secondary

Sushumna-nadi[1] to the head, into the third ventricle of the brain; the eyes glaze, as the life-web draws itself away and the whole of it is collected round the permanent atom in the third ventricle; then the whole rises slowly to the point of junction of the parietal and occipital sutures, and leaves the physical body—dead. It thus surrounds the permanent atom like a golden shell—recalling the closely woven cocoon of the silk-worm—to remain enshrouding it till the building of a new physical body again demands its unfolding. The same procedure is followed with the astral and mental particles, so that when these bodies have disintegrated the lower triad may be seen as a brilliantly scintillating nucleus within the causal body, an appearance which had been noted long ere closer observation revealed its significance.

3. THE CHOOSING OF THE PERMANENT ATOMS

Let us return to the original appropriation by the Monad of the permanent atoms of the three higher planes, and seek to understand something of their use, of the object of their appropriation; the same principles apply to the permanent atoms of each plane.

[1] There is no English name for this passage; it is a vessel, or canal, running from the heart to the third ventricle, and will be familiar under the above name to all students of yoga. The primary Sushumna is the spinal canal.

In the first place, it will be remembered that the matter of each plane shows out seven main types, varying according to the dominance of one or other of the three great attributes of matter: inertia, mobility, and rhythm. Hence the permanent atoms may be chosen out of any one of these types, but it appears that, by a single Monad, they are all chosen out of the same type. It appears, further, that while the actual attachment of the permanent atoms to the life-thread on the three higher planes is the work of the Hierarchies before spoken of, the choice which directs the appropriation is made by the Monad himself. He himself belongs to one or other of the seven groups of Life already spoken of; at the head of each of these groups stands a Planetary Logos, who " colours " the whole, and the Monads are grouped by these colourings, each " being coloured by his ' Father-Star '." [1] This is the first great determining characteristic of each of us, our fundamental " colour", or " key-note", or " temperament ". The Monad may choose to use his new pilgrimage for the strengthening and increasing of this special characteristic; if so, the Hierarchies will attach to his life-thread atoms belonging to the group in matter corresponding to his life-group. This choice would result in the secondary " colour", or " key-note",

[1] See *The Pedigree of Man*, by Annie Besant, p. 24.

or "temperament", emphasising and strengthening the first, and, in the later evolution, the powers and the weaknesses of that doubled temperament would show themselves with great force. Or, the Monad may choose to use his new pilgrimage for the unfolding of another aspect of his nature; then the Hierarchies will attach to his life-thread atoms belonging to the material group corresponding to another life-group, that in which the aspect he wills to develop is predominant. This choice would result in the secondary "colour", or "key-note", or "temperament", modifying the first, with corresponding result in the later evolution. This latter choice is obviously by far the more frequent, and it tends to a greater complexity of character, especially in the final stages of human evolution, when the influence of the Monad makes itself felt more strongly.

As said above, it appears that all the permanent atoms are taken from the same material group, so that those of the lower triad correspond with those of the higher; but on the lower planes the influence of these atoms in determining the type of materials used in the bodies of which they are the generating centres—the question to which we must now turn our attention—is very much limited and interfered with by other causes. On the higher planes the bodies are relatively permanent when once found, and reproduce definitely the key-note of their permanent atoms, however enriched that note may be by overtones ever increasing in subtlety of harmony. But on the lower planes, while the key-note of the permanent atoms will be the same, various other causes come in to determine the choice of materials for the bodies, as will be better seen presently.

4. THE USE OF THE PERMANENT ATOMS

To put this use into a phrase: The use of the permanent atoms is to preserve within themselves, as vibratory powers, the results of all the experiences through which they have passed. It will perhaps be best to take the physical atom as an illustration, since this is susceptible of easier explanation than those on higher planes.

A physical impact of any kind will cause vibrations corresponding to its own in the physical body it contacts; these may be local or general, according to the nature and force of the impact. But whether local or general, they will reach the permanent physical atom, transmitted by the web of life in all cases, and in violent impacts by mere concussion also. This vibration, forced on the atom from outside, becomes a vibratory power in the atom—a tendency therein to repeat the vibration. Through the whole life of the body, innumerable impacts

strike it; not one but leaves its mark on the permanent atom; not one but leaves it with a new possibility of vibration. All the results of physical
experiences remain stored up in this permanent
atom as powers of vibrating. At the end of a
physical life, this permanent atom has thus stored
up innumerable vibratory powers; that is, has
learned to respond in countless ways to the external
world, to reproduce in itself the vibrations imposed
upon it by surrounding objects. The physical
body disintegrates at death; its particles scatter,
all carrying with them the result of the experiences
through which they have passed—as indeed all
particles of our bodies are ever doing day by day,
in their ceaseless dyings out of one body and ceaseless birthings into another. But the physical permanent atom remains; it is the only atom that has
passed through all the experiences of the ever-
changing conglomerations we call our body, and
it has acquired all the results of all those experiences. Wrapped in its golden cocoon it sleeps
through the long years during which the Jivatma
that owns it is living through other experiences in
other worlds. By these it remains unaffected, being
incapable of responding to them, and it sleeps
through its long night in undisturbed repose. [1]

---

[1] H. P. Blavatsky throws out a hint as to these " sleeping atoms ".
See *The Secret Doctrine*, iv, 242, Fifth Adyar Edition.

When the time for reincarnation comes, and the presence of the permanent atom renders possible the fertilization of the ovum from which the new body is to grow,[1] its key-note sounds out, and is one of the forces which guide the ethereal builder, the elemental charged with the building of the physical body, to choose the materials suitable for his work, for he can use none that cannot be to some extent attuned to the permanent atom. But it is only *one* of the forces; the karma of past lives, mental, emotional, and in relation to others, demands materials capable of the most varied expressions; out of that karma, the Lords of Karma have chosen such as is congruous, *i.e.*, such as can be expressed through a body of a particular material group; this congruous mass of karma determines the material group, over-riding the permanent atom, and out of that group are chosen by the elemental such materials as can vibrate in harmony with the permanent atom, or in discords not disruptive in their violence. Hence, as said, the permanent atom is only one of the forces in determining the third " colour", or " key-note", or " temperament", which characterizes each of us. According to this temperament will be the time of the birth of the

[1] H. P. Blavatsky calls the permanent nucleus of the lower $2\frac{1}{2}$ planes " the life-atoms "; she says: " The life-atoms of our (prana) life-principle are never entirely lost when a man dies;" they are " transmitted from father to son." *The Secret Doctrine,* iv, 241 Fifth Adyar Edition.

body; it *must* be born into the world at a time when
the physical planetary influences are suitable to its
third temperament, and it thus is born " under "
its astrological " Star ". Needless to say, it is not
the Star that imposes the temperament, but the
temperament that fixes the epoch of birth under
that Star. But herein lies the explanation of the
correspondences between Stars—Star-Angels, that
is to say—and characters, and the usefulness for
educational purposes of a skillfully and carefully
drawn horoscope, as a guide of the personal temperament of a child.

That such complicated results, capable of im-
pressing their peculiarities on surrounding matter,
can exist in such minute space as an atom may,
indeed, appear inconceivable—yet so it is. And
it is worthy of notice that ordinary science coun-
tenances a similar idea, since the infinitesimal biophors in the germinal cell of Weismann are supposed to thus carry on to the offspring the characteristics of his line of progenitors. While the one
brings to the body its physical peculiarities from its
ancestors, the other supplies those which have been
acquired by the evolving man during his own
evolution. H. P. Blavatsky has put this very
clearly:

" The German embryologist-philosopher—step-
ping over the heads of the Greek Hippocrates and

Aristotle, right back into the teachings of the old Aryans—shows one infinitesimal cell, out of millions of others at work in the formation of an organism, alone and unaided determining, by means of constant segmentation and multiplication, the correct image of the future man, or animal, in its physical, mental and psychic characteristics. . . . Complete the physical plasm, mentioned above, the ' germinal cell ' of man with all its material potentialities, with the ' spiritual plasm ', so to say, or the fluid that contains the five lower principles of the six-principled Dhyani—and you have the secret, if you are spiritual enough to understand it." [1]

A little study of physical heredity in the light of Weismann's teachings will be sufficient to convince the student of the possibilities of such a body as the permanent atom. A man reproduces the features of a long-past ancestor, shows out a physical peculiarity that characterized a forbear several centuries ago. We can trace the Stuart nose through a long series of portraits, and innumerable cases of such resemblances can be found. Why, then, should there be anything extraordinary in the idea that an atom should gather within itself not biophors, as in the germinal cell, but tendencies to repeat innumerable vibrations already practised? No spatial difficulty arises, any more than in the

[1] *The Secret Doctrine*, i, 270, Fifth Adyar Edition.

case of a string, from which numerous notes can be drawn by bowing it at different points, each note containing numerous overtones. We must not think of the minute space of an atom as crowded with innumerable vibrating bodies, but of a limited number of bodies, each capable of setting up innumerable vibrations.

Truly, however, even the spatial difficulty is illusory, for there are no limits to the minute any more than to the great. Modern science now sees in the atom a system of revolving worlds, each world in its own orbit, the whole resembling a solar system. The master of illusion, Space, like his brother master, Time, cannot here daunt us. There is no limit to the possibilities of sub-division in thought, and hence none in the thought-expression we call matter.

The normal number of spirillæ at work in the permanent atoms in this Round is four, as in the ordinary unattached atoms of matter in general at this stage of evolution. But let us take the permanent atom in the body of a very highly evolved man, a man far in advance of his fellows. In such a case we may find the permanent atom showing five spirillæ at work, and may seek to learn the bearing of this fact on the general materials of his body. In ante-natal life, the presence of this five-spirillæ-permanent-atom would have caused the building elemental to select among his materials any similar atoms that were available. For the most part, he would be reduced to the use of any he could find, which had been in temporary connection with any body the centre of which was a five-spirillæ permanent atom. Its presence would have tended to arouse in them a corresponding activity, especially—perhaps only—if they had formed part of the brain or nerves of the highly developed tenant of the body. The fifth spirilla would have become more or less active in them, and although it would have dropped back into inactivity after leaving such a body, its temporary activity would have predisposed it to respond more readily in the future to the current of monadic life. Such atoms, then, would be secured by the elemental for his work, as far as possible. He would also, should opportunity serve, appropriate from the paternal or maternal bodies, if they were of a high order, any such atoms as he could secure, and build them into his charge. After birth, and throughout life, such a body would attract to itself any similar atoms which come within its magnetic field. Such a body, in the company of highly evolved persons, would profit to an exceptional degree by the propinquity, appropriating any five-spirillæ atoms which were present in the shower of particles flung off from their bodies, and thus gaining physically

6

as well as mentally and morally, from their company.

The permanent astral atom bears exactly the same relation to the astral body as that borne by the physical permanent atom to the physical body. At the end of the life in kamaloka—purgatory—the golden life-web withdraws from the astral body, leaving it to disintegrate, as its physical comrade had previously done, and enwraps the astral permanent atom for its long sleep. A similar relation is borne to the mental body by the permanent mental particle during physical, astral, and mental life; during the early stages of human evolution little improvement is made in the mental permanent unit by the brief devachanic lives, not only on account of their brevity, but because the feeble thought-forms produced by the undeveloped intelligence affect very slightly the permanent unit. But when thought-power is more highly evolved, the devachanic life is a time of great improvement, and innumerable vibratory energies are stored up, and show their value when the time arrives for the building of a new mental body for the next cycle of reincarnation. At the close of the mental life in devachan the golden web withdraws from the mental body, leaving it also to disintegrate, while it enwraps the mental particle; and the lower triad of permanent atoms alone remains as the representative of the three lower bodies. These are stored up, as before said, as a radiant nucleus-like particle within the causal body. They are thus all that remains to the Ego of his bodies in the lower worlds, when that cycle of experience is completed, as they were his means of communication with the lower planes during the life of those bodies.

When comes the period for rebirth, a thrill of life from the Ego arouses the mental unit; the life-web begins to unfold again, and the vibrating unit acts as a magnet, drawing towards itself materials with vibratory powers resembling, or accordant with, its own. The Shining Ones of the Second Elemental Kingdom bring such materials within its reach; in the earlier stages of evolution they shape the matter into a loose cloud around the permanent unit, but as evolution goes on the Ego exercises over the shaping an ever-increasing influence. When the mental body is partially formed, the life-thrill awakens the astral atom, and the same procedure is followed. Finally the life-touch reaches the physical atom, and it acts in the way already described on pp. 77-79.

A questioner sometimes asks: How can these permanent atoms be stored up within the causal body, without losing their physical, astral, and mental natures, since the causal body exists on a higher plane, where the physical, as physical, cannot be?

Such a querent is forgetting, for a moment, that all the planes are interpenetrating, and that it is no more difficult for the causal body to encircle the triad of the lower planes, than for it to encircle the hundreds of millions of atoms that form the mental, astral, and physical bodies belonging to it during a period of earth-life. The triad forms a minute particle within the causal body; each constituent part of it belongs to its own plane, but, as the planes have meeting points everywhere, no difficulty arises in the necessary juxtaposition. We are all on all planes at all times.

5.   MONADIC ACTION ON THE PERMANENT ATOMS

We may here enquire: Is there anything that can be properly termed monadic action—the action of the Monad on the anupadaka plane—on the permanent atom? Of direct action there is none, nor can there be until the germinal spiritual Triad has reached a high stage of evolution; indirect action, that is action on the spiritual Triad, which in turn acts on the lower, there is continually. But for all practical purposes we may consider it as the action of the spiritual Triad, which, as we have seen, is the Monad veiled in matter denser than that of his native plane.

The spiritual Triad is drawing most of his energy, and all the directive capacity of that energy, from the Second Logos, bathed as he is in that stream of Life. What may be called his own special activity does not concern itself with all the shaping and building activity of the second Life-Wave, but is directed to the evolution of the atom itself, in association with the Third Logos. This energy from the spiritual Triad confines itself to the atomic sub-planes, and until the fourth Round appears to spend itself chiefly on the permanent atoms. It is directed first to the shaping and then to the vivifying of the spirillæ which form the wall of the atom. The vortex, which is the atom, is the life of the Third Logos; but the wall of the spirillæ is gradually formed on the external surface of this vortex during the descent of the Second Logos, not vivified by Him, but faintly traced out over the surface of this revolving vortex of life. They remain—so far as the Second Logos is concerned—merely as these filmy unused channels, but presently, as the life of the Monad flows down, it plays into the first of these channels, vivifying that channel and turning it into a working part of the atom. This goes on through the successive Rounds, and by the time we reach the fourth Round we have four distinct streams of life from each Monad, circulating through four sets of spirillæ in his own permanent atoms.

Now as the Monad works in the permanent atom, and it is put forward as the nucleus of a body, he begins to work similarly in the atoms that are drawn round that permanent atom, and vivifies in turn their spirillæ; but that is temporary vivification, and not continuous as in the case of the permanent atom. He thus brings into activity these faint shadowy films, formed by the Second Life-Wave, and, when the life of the body is broken up, the atoms thus stimulated return to the great mass of atomic matter, improved and worked upon by the life which, during their connection with the permanent atom, has been vivifying them. The channels, being thus developed, are more capable of easily receiving another such life-stream as they enter another body and therein come into relation with a permanent atom belonging to some other Monad. Thus this work continually goes on, on the physical and astral planes and in the particle of mental matter on the mental plane, improving the materials with which the Monads are permanently or temporarily connected, and this evolution of atoms is constantly going on under the influence of the Monads. The permanent atoms evolve more rapidly because of their continuity of connection with the Monad, while the others profit by their repeated temporary association with the permanent atoms.

During the first Round of the terrene Chain, the
first set of spirillæ of the physical plane atoms
becomes thus vivified by the life of the Monad
flowing through the spiritual Triad. This is the
set of spirillæ used by the pranic, or life-breath,
currents affecting the dense part of the physical
body. Similarly, in the second Round the second
set of spirillæ becomes active, and herein play the
pranic currents connected with the etheric double.
During these two Rounds nothing can be found, in
connection with any form, that can be called sensations of pleasure and pain. During the third
Round, the third set of spirillæ becomes vivified,
and here first appears what is called sensibility; for
through these spirillæ kamic or desire energy can
affect the physical body, the kamic prana can play
in them, and thus bring the physical into direct
communication with the astral. During the fourth
Round, the fourth set of spirillæ becomes vivified,
and the kama-manasic prana plays in them, and
makes them fit to be used for the building of a brain
which is to act as the instrument for thought.

When a person passes out of the normal, and
takes up the abnormal human evolution involved
in preparing for and entering the Path which lies
beyond normal evolution, he has then, in connection with his permanent atoms, a task of exceeding
difficulty. He must vivify more sets of spirillæ than

are vivified in the humanity of his time.   Four sets
are already at his service, as a fourth Round man.
He begins to vivify a fifth, and thus to bring into
manifestation the fifth Round atom while still
working in a fourth Round body.   It is to this that
allusion is made in some early Theosophical books,
in which " Fifth Rounders " and " Sixth Rounders "
are spoken of as appearing in our present humanity.
Those thus designated have evolved the fifth and
sixth set of spirillæ in their permanent atoms, thus
obtaining a better instrument for the use of their
highly developed consciousness. The change is
brought about by certain yoga practices in the use
of which great caution is required, lest injury should
be inflicted on the brain in which this work is being
carried on, and further progress along that particular line stopped during the present incarnation.

CHAPTER V

GROUP-SOULS

1. THE MEANING OF THE TERM

SPEAKING generally, a Group-Soul is a collection of permanent triads, in a triple envelope of monadic essence. The description is true of all Group-Souls functioning on the physical plane, but gives no idea of the extreme complexity of the subject of Group-Souls. For they divide and subdivide constantly, the contents of each division and sub-division decreasing in number, as evolution goes on, until at last a " Group-Soul " encloses but a single triad, to which it may continue for many births to discharge the protective and nutrient functions of a Group-Soul while no longer technically describable as one, the " Group " having separated off into its constituent parts.

Seven Group-Souls are to be seen, functioning on the physical plane, before any forms appear. They first show themselves as vague, filmy forms, one in each stream of the Second Life-Wave, on the mental plane, becoming more clearly outlined on the astral plane, and yet more so on the physical. They float in the great ocean of matter as balloons might float in the sea. Observing them more closely, we see three separate layers of matter, forming an envelope, which contains innumerable triads. Before any inmineralization has taken place, no golden life-web is, of course, visible around these; only the radiant golden threads which connect them with their parent Jivatmas are to be seen, shining with that strange lustre which belongs to their birth-plane. The innermost of these three layers consists of physical monadic essence; that is, the layer is composed of atoms of the physical plane, ensouled with the life of the Second Logos. At first sight, these innermost layers appear to be identical in the seven Group-Souls; but closer observation reveals that each layer is formed of atoms from only one of the seven Matter-groups before described. Each Group-Soul, therefore, differs in material constitution from all the rest, and the contained triads in each belong to the same matter-group. The second layer of the Group-Soul envelope is composed of astral monadic essence, belonging to the same matter-group as the first; and the third of units of the fourth sub-plane of mental matter of the same type. This triple envelope is the protector and nourisher of the triads contained within it, veritable embryos, incapable, as yet, of separate independent activity.

The seven Group-Souls soon multiply, division going on continually with the multiplication of distinct sub-types, as the immediate forerunners of the chemical elements appear, to be followed by the elements themselves and the minerals formed from them. The laws of space, for instance—apart from the specialization of the contents of the Group-Soul, the permanent triads—may lead to a division of it.

Thus a vein of gold in Australia may lead to the inmineralization of many such triads within a single envelope, while the laying down of another vein in a distant place, say the Rocky Mountains, may lead to the division of this envelope and the transfer of part of its contents to America in their own envelope. But the more important causes which bring about subdivisions will be explained in the course of our study. The Group-Soul and its contents divide by fission, like an ordinary cell—one becomes two, two four, and so on. All the triads have to pass through the mineral kingdom, the place in which matter reaches its grossest form, and the place where the great wave reaches the limit of its descent and turns to begin its upward climbing. Here it is that physical consciousness must awaken; life must now turn definitely outwards, and recognize contact with other lives in an external world.

Now the evolution of each being in these early stages depends chiefly on the cherishing life of the Logos, and partly on the cooperating guidance of the Shining Ones, and partly on its own blind pressure against the limits of its enclosing form. I have compared the evolution through the mineral, vegetable, and animal kingdoms to an ante-natal period, and the resemblance is exact. As the child is nourished by the life-streams of the mother, so does the protective envelope of the Group-Soul nourish the lives within it, receiving and distributing the experiences gathered in. The circulating life is the life of the parent; the young plants, the young animals, the young human beings, are not ready for independent life as yet, but must draw nourishment from the parent. And so these germinating lives in the mineral kingdom are nourished by the Group-Souls, by the envelopes of monadic essence, thrilling with Logic life. A very fair picture of this stage may be seen in the carpel of a plant, in which the ovules gradually appear, becoming more and more independent.

For the sake of a clear conception, we may glance rapidly forward over the changes through which the Group-Soul passes, as its contents evolve, before going into details. During the mineral evolution, the habitat of the Group-Soul may be said to be that of its densest envelope, the physical; its most active working is on the physical plane. As its contents pass onwards into the vegetable kingdom, and ascend through it, the physical envelope slowly disappears—as though absorbed by the contents for the strengthening of their own etheric bodies—and its activity is transferred to the astral plane, to the nourishing of the astral bodies of the contained triads. As these develop yet further and pass into the animal kingdom, the astral envelope is similarly absorbed, and the activity of the Group-Soul is transferred to the mental plane, and it nourishes the inchoate mental bodies and shapes them gradually into less vagueness of outline. When the Group-Soul contains but a single triad, and has nourished this into readiness for the reception of the third outpouring, what is left of it disintegrates into matter of the third sub-plane and becomes a constituent part of the causal body formed by the downpouring from above meeting the upward-drawn column from below—to use the graphic water-spout simile. Then is the reincarnating Ego born into independent manifestation; the guarded ante-natal life is over.

2. THE DIVISION OF THE GROUP-SOUL

It is on the physical plane that consciousness must first evolve into Self-consciousness, must become aware of an external world that makes impacts upon it, and must learn to refer those impacts to an external world and to realize as its own the changes which it undergoes in consequence of those impacts. By prolonged experiences it will learn to identify with itself the feeling of pleasure or pain that follows the impact, and to regard as not itself that which touches its external surface. It will thus make its first rough distinction of " Not-I " and " I ". As experience increase, the " I " will retreat ever inwards, and one veil of matter after another will be relegated outwards as belonging to the " Not-I "; but while its connotations change, this fundamental distinction between subject and object will ever remain. " I " is the willing, thinking, acting consciousness; while the " Not-I " is all as to which it wills, about which it thinks, and on which it acts. We shall have to consider later the way in which consciousness becomes Self-consciousness, but at present we are concerned only with its expression in forms and the part played by the forms.

This consciousness awakens on the physical plane, and its expression is the permanent atom. In this it lies sleeping: " It sleeps in the mineral "; and therein some awakening into lighter slumber must take place, so that it may be roused out of this deep dreamless sleep and become sufficiently active to pass on into the next stage: " It dreams in the vegetable."

Now the Second Logos, acting in the envelope of the Group-Souls, energizes the permanent physical atoms and, by the mediation of the Shining Ones as we have seen, plunges them into the various conditions offered by the mineral kingdom, where each attaches to itself many mineral particles. At once here we see a large variety of possible impacts, leading to a variety of experiences, and so presently to lines of cleavage in a Group-Soul. Some will be whirled high in air, to fall in torrents of burning lava; some will be exposed to arctic cold, others to tropic heat; some will be crushed and sheathed in molten metal, in the bowels of the earth; some will be in the sand tossed roughly by rushing billows. Infinite variety of external impacts will shake and strike and burn and freeze, and in vague answers of sympathetic vibrations will the deep-slumbering consciousness respond. When any permanent atom has reached a certain responsiveness, or when a mineral form, *i.e.*, the particles to which a permanent atom has attached itself, is broken up, the Group-Soul draws that atom from its encasement. All the experiences acquired by that atom—and that means the vibrations it has been forced to execute—remain as powers of vibrating in particular ways, or as " vibratory-powers ". That is the outcome of its life in a form. The permanent atom, losing its embodiment and remaining for a while naked, as it were, in its Group-Soul, and continuing to repeat these vibrations, to go over within itself its life-experiences, sets up pulses which run through the envelope of the Group-Soul and are thus conveyed to other permanent atoms: thus each affects and helps all the others while remaining itself. The permanent atoms which have had experiences similar in character will be more strongly affected by each other than will be those whose experiences have been very different, and thus there will be a certain segregation going on within the Group-Soul, and presently a filmy separating wall will grow inwards from the envelope and divide these segregated groups from each other; and so there will be an ever increasing number of Group-Souls with contents showing an ever-increasing distinction of consciousness, while sharing fundamental characteristics.

Now the responses of consciousness to external stimuli in the mineral kingdom are far greater than many quite realize, and some of them are of a nature which shows that there is a dawning of consciousness also in the astral permanent atom. For chemical elements exhibit distinct mutual attractions, and chemical marital relationships are continually disorganized by the intrusion of couples, one or other of which has a stronger affinity for one of the partners in the earlier marriage than the original mate. Thus a hitherto mutually faithful couple, forming a silver salt, will suddenly prove faithless to each other if another couple, hydrochloric acid, enters their peaceful household; and the silver will pounce upon the chlorine and take her to wife, preferring her to his former mate, and set up a new household as silver chloride, leaving the deserted hydrogen to mate with his own forsaken partner. Wherever these active interchanges go on there is a slight stir in the astral atom, in consequence of the violent physical vibrations set up by the violent wrenching apart, and formation of intimate ties, and vague internal thrillings appear. The astral must be roused from the physical, and consciousness on the physical plane will long take the lead in evolution. Still, a little cloud of astral matter is drawn round the permanent astral atom by these slight thrillings, but it is very loosely held and seems to be quite unorganized. There does not seem to be any vibration in the mental atom at this stage.

After ages of experience in the mineral kingdom, some of the permanent atoms will be ready to pass into the vegetable kingdom, and will be distributed by the agency of the Shining Ones over the vegetable world. It is not to be supposed that every blade of grass, every plant, has a permanent atom

7

within it, evolving to humanity during the life of this system. Just as in the mineral kingdom, so here; the vegetable kingdom forms the field of evolution for these permanent atoms, and the Shining Ones guide them to habitat after habitat, so that they may experience the vibrations that affect the vegetable world, and again store up these as vibratory powers in the same fashion as before. The principles of interchange and of consequent segregation work out as before, and the Group-Souls in each stream of evolution become more numerous, and more different in their leading characteristics.

At our present stage of knowledge, the laws according to which permanent atoms in a Group-Soul are plunged into the kingdoms of nature are by no means clear. Many things seem to indicate that the evolution of the mineral, vegetable, and the lowest part of the animal kingdom belong more to the evolution of the earth itself than to that of the Jivatmas representing the Monads who are evolving within the solar system, and who come, in due course, to this earth to pursue their own evolution by utilizing the conditions it affords. Grass and small plants of every kind seem to be related to the earth as a man's hairs are related to his body and not to be connected with the Monads, represented by Jivatmas in our fivefold universe. The life in them, holding them together as forms, appears to be that of the Second Logos, and the life in the atoms and molecules composing them to be that of the Third Logos, appropriated and modified by the Planetary Logos of our system of Chains, and further appropriated and modified by the Spirit of the Earth—an entity wrapped in great obscurity. These kingdoms offer a field for the evolution of the Jivatmas truly, but do not exist, apparently, wholly for this purpose. We find permanent atoms scattered through the mineral and vegetable kingdoms, but are unable to pierce to the reasons which govern their distribution. A permanent atom may be found in a pearl, in a ruby, in a diamond; many may be found scattered through veins of ore, and so on. On the other hand much mineral does not seem to contain any. So with short-lived plants. But in plants of long continuance, such as trees, permanent atoms are constantly found. But here again, the life of the tree seems to be more closely related to the Deva-evolution than to the evolution of the consciousness to which the permanent atom is attached. It is rather as though advantage were taken of the evolution of life and consciousness in the tree for the benefit of the permanent atom: it seems to live there more as a parasite, profiting by the more highly evolved life in which it is bathed. The fact is that our knowledge on these points is extremely fragmentary so far.

There is more activity perceptible in the astral permanent atom during the course of the accumulation of vegetable experiences by the physical, and it attracts round itself astral matter which is arranged by the Shining Ones in a rather more definite way. In the long life of a forest tree, the growing aggregation of astral matter develops itself in all directions as the astral form of the tree, and the consciousness attached to the permanent atoms shares, to some extent, that of its surroundings, experiencing through that astral form the vibrations causing massive pleasure and discomfort, these vibrations being the result of those set up in the physical tree by sunshine and storm, wind and rain, cold and heat. With the perishing of such a tree, the permanent astral atom retreats to its Group-Soul, now established on the astral plane with a rich store of experiences, shared in the manner before described.

Further, as the consciousness becomes more responsive in the astral, it sends little thrills downwards to the physical plane, and these give rise to feelings felt as though in the physical, but really derived from the astral. Where there has been a long separate life, as in a tree, the permanent mental unit will also begin to attract round itself a little cloud of mental matter, and on this the recurrence of seasons will slowly impress itself as a faint memory, which becomes inevitably a faint anticipation.[1]

At last some of the permanent physical atoms are ready to pass on into the animal kingdom, and once more the agency of the Shining Ones guides them into animal forms. During the later stages of their evolution in the vegetable world, it appears to be the rule that each triad—physical and astral atoms and mental unit—shall have a prolonged experience in a single form, so that some thrills of mental life may be experienced, and the triad may thus be prepared to profit by the wandering life of the animal. But it also appears that in some cases the passage into the animal kingdom is made at an earlier stage, and that the first thrill in the mental unit occurs in some of the stationary forms of animal life, and in very lowly animal organisms.

In the lowest types of animals conditions similar to those described as existing in the mineral and vegetable kingdoms also appear to prevail. Microbes, amœbæ, hydræ, etc., etc., only show a permanent atom as a visitor, now and again, and obviously in no way depend upon it for life and growth, nor do they break up when the permanent atom is withdrawn. They are hosts, not bodies formed around a permanent atom. And it is noteworthy that, at

---

[1] See *Thought-Power, Its Control and Culture*, by Annie Besant, pp. 59-62.

this stage, the golden life-web in no way represents
the organization of the host's body, but merely acts
as rootlets act in the soil, attaching particles of soil
to themselves and sucking therefrom nourishment.
The permanent atoms in the animal kingdom have
received and stored up many experiences before
they are used by the Shining Ones as centres round
which forms are to be built.

Needless to say that in the animal kingdom the
permanent atoms receive far more varied vibrations
than in the lower kingdoms, and consequently
differentiate more quickly, the number of triads in
the Group-Soul diminishing rapidly as this differentiation proceeds and the multiplication of Group-
Souls therefore going on with increasing rapidity.
As the period of individuality approaches, each
separate triad becomes possessed of its own envelope,
obtained from the Group-Soul, and takes on successive embodiments as a separate entity, though still
within the enveloping case of protecting and
nourishing monadic essence.

Large numbers of the higher animals in a state of
domestication have reached this stage, and have
really become separate reincarnating entities, although not as yet possessing a causal body—the
mark of what is usually called individualization.
The envelope derived from the Group-Soul serves
the purpose of a causal body, but consists only of

the third layer, as previously indicated, and is therefore composed of molecules derived from the fourth
grade of mental matter, that which corresponds to
the coarsest ether of the physical plane. Following
the analogy of human ante-natal life, we see that
this stage corresponds with its last two months. A
seven-months' babe may be born and may survive,
but it will be stronger, healthier, more vigorous,
if it profits for yet another two months by its
mother's shielding and nourishing life. So it is
better for the normal development of the Ego that
it should not too hastily burst the envelope of the
Group-Soul, but should still absorb life through it,
and strengthen from its constituents the finest part
of its own mental body. When that body has
reached its limit of growth under these shielded
conditions, the envelope disintegrates into the finer
molecules of the sub-plane above it, and becomes,
as abovesaid, part of the causal body.

It is the knowledge of these facts that has sometimes caused occultists to warn people who are very
fond of animals not to be exaggerated in their
affection, nor to show it in unwise ways. The
growth of the animal may be unhealthily forced,
and its birth into individuality be hastened out of
due time. Man, in order to fill rightly his place in
the world, should seek to understand nature and
work with her laws, quickening indeed their action

by the co-operation of his intelligence, but not quickening it to the point whereat growth is made unhealthy and its product frail and " out of season ". It is true that the Lord of Life seeks human co-operation in the working out of evolution, but the co-operation should follow the lines which His Wisdom has laid down.

CHAPTER VI

UNITY OF CONSCIOUSNESS

1. CONSCIOUSNESS A UNIT

IN studying the very varied manifestations of consciousness, we are apt to forget two important facts: first, that the consciousness of each man is a Unit, however separate and different from each other its manifestations may appear to be; secondly, that all these Units themselves are parts of the consciousness of the Logos, and therefore react similarly under similar conditions. We cannot too often remind ourselves that consciousness is one; that all apparently separate consciousnesses are truly one, as one sea might pour through many holes in an embankment. That sea-water might issue from the holes differently coloured, if the embankment were composed of differently coloured earths; but it would all be the same sea-water; analysed, it would all show the presence of the same characteristic salts. So are all consciousnesses from the same ocean of consciousness, and have many essential identities. Enveiled in the same kind of matter, they will act in the same kind of way, and reveal their fundamental identity of nature.

The individual consciousness appears to be a complexity instead of a unity when its manifestations are concerned, and modern psychology speaks of dual and treble and multiplex personality, losing sight of the fundamental unity among the confusion of the manifold. Yet truly is our consciousness a Unit, and the variety is due to the materials in which it is working.

The ordinary waking-consciousness of a man is the consciousness working through the physical brain at a certain rate imposed by it, conditioned by all the conditions of that brain, limited by all its limitations, baulked by the varying obstructions it offers, checked by a clot of blood, silenced by the decay of tissue. At every moment the brain hinders its manifestations, while at the same time it is, on the physical plane, its only enabling instrument of manifestation.

When the consciousness, turning its attention away from the external physical world, ignores the denser part of the physical brain, and uses only the etheric portions thereof, its manifestations at once change in character. The creative imagination disports itself in etheric matter, and drawing on its accumulated contents, obtained from the external world by its denser servant, it arranges them, dissociates, and recombines them after its own fancies, and creates the lower worlds of dream.

When it casts aside for a while its ethereal garment, turning its attention away completely from the physical world and shedding its fetters of physical matter, it roams through the astral world at will, or drifts through it unconsciously, turning all its attention to its own contents, receiving many impacts from that astral world, which it ignores or accepts according to its stage of evolution or its humour of the moment. If it should manifest itself to an outside observer—as may happen in trance-conditions—it shows powers so superior to those it manifested when imprisoned in the physical brain, that such an observer, judging only by physical experiences, may well regard it as a different consciousness.

Still more is this the case when, the astral body being thrown into trance, the Bird of Heaven shows itself soaring into loftier regions, and its splendid flight so enchants the observer that he deems it a new being, and no longer the same entity as crawled in the physical world. Yet truly is it ever one and the same; the differences are in the materials with which it is connected and through which it works, and not in itself.

As to the second important fact stated above, man is not yet sufficiently developed to appreciate any evidence as to the unity of consciousness in its workings above the physical plane, but its unity on the physical plane is being demonstrated.

2.   UNITY OF PHYSICAL CONSCIOUSNESS

Amid the immense varieties of the mineral, vegetable, animal, and human kingdoms, the underlying unity of physical consciousness has been lost sight of, and broad lines of cleavage have been set up which do not, in reality, exist. Life has been wholly denied to the mineral, grudged to the vegetable, and H. P. Blavatsky was ridiculed when she declared that one Life, one Consciousness, vivified and informed all.

" With every day, the identity between the animal and the physical man, between the plant and man, and even between the reptile and its nest, the rock, and man, is more and more clearly shown, the physical and chemical constituents of all being found to be identical. Chemical Science may well say that there is no difference between the matter which composes the ox, and that which forms man. But the occult doctrine is far more explicit. It says: Not only the chemical compounds are the same, but the same infinitesimal invisible Lives compose the atoms of the bodies of the mountain and the daisy, of man and the ant, of the elephant and of the tree which shelters it from the sun. Each particle—whether you call it organic or inorganic —is a Life." [1]

If this be true, it should be possible to obtain from such living minerals, vegetables, animals, and men, evidence of an identity of life, of sentiency, of response to stimuli; and while we may freely admit that we should expect to find gradations of sentiency, that as we ascend the ladder of life we should expect the manifestations to become fuller and more complex, yet some definite manifestations of sentiency should be found in all who share one life. The evidence for this was lacking when H. P. Blavatsky wrote; it is available now; and it is from an eastern scientist, whose rare ability has ensured his welcome in the West, that the evidence appropriately comes.

Professor Jagadish Chandra Bose, M.A., D.SC., of Calcutta, has definitely proved that so-called "inorganic matter" is responsive to stimulus, and that the response is identical from metals, vegetables, animals, and—so far as experiment can be made—man.

He arranged apparatus to measure the stimulus applied, and to show in curves, traced on a revolving cylinder, the response from the body receiving the stimulus. He then compared the curves obtained

[1] *The Secret Doctrine*, I. 304, Fifth Adyar Edition.

in tin and in other metals with those obtained from muscle, and found that the curves from tin were identical with those from muscle, and that other metals gave curves of like nature but varied in the period of recovery.

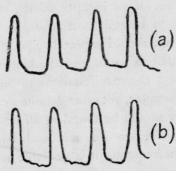

(a) Series of electric responses to successive mechanical stimuli at intervals of half a minute, in tin. (b) Mechanical responses in muscle.

Tetanus, both complete and incomplete, due to repeated shocks, was caused and similar results accrued, in mineral as in muscle.

Fatigue was shown by metals, least of all by tin. Chemical reagents, such as drugs, produced similar results on metals with those known to result with animals—exciting, depressing, and deadly. (By deadly is meant resulting in the destruction of the power of response.)

A poison will kill a metal, inducing a condition of immobility, so that no response is obtainable. If the poisoned metal be taken in time, an antidote may save its life.

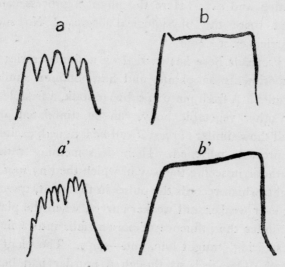

Effects analogous to (*a*) incomplete and (*b*) complete tetanus in tin, (*a'*) incomplete and (*b'*) complete tetanus in muscle.

(*a*) Normal response.   (*b*) Effect of poison.   (*c*) Revival by antidote.

A stimulant will increase response, and as large and small doses of a drug have been found to kill and stimulate respectively, so have they been found to act on metals. "Among such phenomena," asks Professor Bose, "how can we draw a line of demarcation and say: 'Here the physical process ends, and there the physiological begins'? No such barriers exist."[1]

Professor Bose has carried on a similar series of experiments on plants, and has obtained similar results. A fresh piece of cabbage stalk, a fresh leaf, or other vegetable body, can be stimulated and will show similar curves; it can be fatigued, excited, depressed, poisoned. There is something rather pathetic in seeing the way in which the tiny spot of light, which records the pulses in the plant, travels, in ever weaker and weaker curves, when the plant is under the influence of poison, falls into a final despairing straight line, and—stops. The plant is dead. One feels as though a murder had been committed—as indeed it has.[2]

These admirable series of experiments have established, on a definite basis of physical facts, the teaching of occult science on the universality of life.

Mr. Marcus Reed has made microscopical observations which show the presence of consciousness in

[1] These details are taken from a paper given by Professor Bose at the Royal Institute, May 10th, 1901, entitled "The Response of Inorganic Matter to Stimulus".

[2] The Professor has not published this lecture, but the facts are in his book *Response in the Living and Non-Living*. I had the good fortune to see the experiments repeated at his own house, where one could watch them closely.

the vegetable kingdom. He has observed symptoms as of fright when tissue is injured, and further he has seen that male and female cells, floating in the sap, become aware of each other's presence without contact; the circulation quickens, and they put out processes towards each other.[1]

More than three years after the publication of Professor Bose's experiments, some interesting confirmation of his observations arose in the course of M. Jean Becquerel's study of the N-rays, communicated by him to the Paris Academy of Sciences. Animals under chloroform cease to emit these rays, and they are never emitted by a corpse. Flowers normally emit them, but under chloroform the emanation ceases. Metals also emit them, and under chloroform the emanation again ceases. Thus animals, flowers, and metals alike give out these rays, and alike cease to emanate them under the action of chloroform.[2]

3. The Meaning of Physical Consciousness

The term "physical consciousness" is used in two distinct senses, and it may be useful to pause a

[1] " Consciousness in Vegetable Matter "; *Pall Mall Magazine*; June, 1902.
[2] The N-rays are due to vibrations in the etheric double, causing waves in the surrounding ether. Chloroform expels the etheric double, and hence the waves cease. At death, the etheric double leaves the body, and the rays consequently can no longer be observed.

moment, in order to define these. It is often used to indicate what is above termed " ordinary waking-consciousness," *i.e.*, the consciousness of the man, of the Jivatma—or, if the phrase be preferred, of the Monad working through the Jivatma and the lower triad of permanent atoms. It is also used in the sense in which it is used here, as consciousness working in physical matter, receiving and responding to physical impacts, unconcerned with any transmission of impulses onward to the higher planes, or with any impulses sent to the physical body from those planes.

In this more restricted and accurate sense, it would include: (*a*) any out-thrillings from the atoms and molecules ensouled by the life of the Third Logos; (*b*) any similar out-thrillings from organized forms ensouled by the life of the Second Logos; and (*c*) any similar out-thrillings from the life of the Monad, proceeding from the permanent atoms, in which the spirillæ are not directly concerned. When the spirillæ are active, the " ordinary waking-consciousness " is affected. For instance, ammonia sniffed up by the nose shows two results: there is a rapid secretion; *that* is the response of the cells in the olfactory tract; there is also a " smell "; *that* is the result of a vibration running up to the sense-centres in the astral body, and there recognized in consciousness; the change in consciousness affects the first set of spirillæ in the atoms of the olfactory tract, and thus reaches the "waking-consciousness"—consciousness working in the physical brain. It is only through the spirillæ that changes in consciousness on the higher planes bring about changes in the " waking-consciousness ".

It must be remembered that as the solar system is a field for the evolution of all the developing consciousness within it, so are there smaller areas within it, serving as smaller fields. Man is the microcosm of the universe, and his body serves as a field of evolution for myriads of consciousnesses less evolved than his own. Thus the three activities mentioned above under (a), (b), and (c) are all present in his body, and all enter into the physical consciousness working therein; that in which the atomic spirillæ are concerned does not enter it; that belongs to the consciousness of the Jivatma. The workings of physical consciousness do not now directly affect the " waking-consciousness " in the higher animals or in man. They affected it in the earlier part of the embryonic life in the Group-Soul, while the consciousness in the Second Logos was " mothering " the dawning consciousness derived from it. But physical consciousness has now sunk below the " threshold of consciousness", while showing itself as " the memory of the cell " as the selective action in glands and papillæ, and generally in the carrying on of functions necessary for the support of bodies. It is the lowest activity of consciousness, and (as consciousness functions more and more actively on the higher plane), its lowest workings no longer attract its attention, and they become what we call automatic.

Now, it is physical consciousness that is appealed to in Professor Bose's experiments, and it is the response of this consciousness in the tin and in the animal that is the same, and is shown in the pulse indicated by the curves; the animal will feel the stimulus while the tin will not—that is the result of the additional working of the consciousness in astral matter.

We may thus allege that consciousness, working in physical matter, responds to various kinds of stimulation, and that the response is the same, whether it be obtained from mineral, vegetable, or animal. The consciousness shows the same characteristic workings, *is* the same. The differences which, as already said, we observe as we ascend, lie in the improvement of the physical apparatus, an apparatus which enables astral and mental—not physical—activities of consciousness to manifest themselves on the physical plane. Men and animals feel and think better than minerals and vegetables, because their more highly evolved consciousness has shaped for itself on the physical plane this much improved apparatus; but even so, our bodies answer as the lower bodies answer to the same stimuli, and this purely physical consciousness is the same in all.

Now in the mineral, the astral matter connected with the permanent astral atom is so little active, and consciousness is sleeping so deeply therein, that there is no perceptible working from the astral to the physical. In the higher plants there seems to be a sort of forthshadowing of a nervous system, but it is too little developed and organized to serve anything but the simplest purposes. The added activity on the astral plane improves the astral sheath in connection with the plant, and the vibrations of the astral sheath affect the etheric portion of the plant, and thus its denser matter. Hence the forthshadowing of a nervous system alluded to above.

When we come to the animal stage, the much greater activity of the consciousness on the astral plane causes more powerful vibrations, which pass to the etheric double of the animal, and by the etheric vibrations thus caused, the nervous system is builded. The shaping of it is due to the Logos through the Group-Soul, and to the active assistance of the Shining Ones of the Third Elemental Kingdom, directing the work of the ethereal Nature-Spirits. But the impulse comes from the consciousness on the astral plane working in the permanent atom and the sheath of astral matter attracted by it, roused to activity by the Group-Soul. As the first very simple apparatus is formed, more delicate impacts from without can be perceived, and these impacts also help in the evolution. Action and reaction succeed each other, and the mechanism continually improves in receptive and transmitting ability.

Consciousness does not do much building on the astral plane at this stage, and works there in an unorganized sheath; the organizing is done on the physical plane by the efforts of consciousness to express itself—dim and vaguely grouping as these efforts are—aided and directed by the Group-Soul and the Shining Ones. This work has to be completed to a great extent before the Third Life-Wave pours down, for " animal man " has evolved, with his brain and nervous systems, before that great outpouring comes which gives the Jivatma a working body and makes possible the higher evolution of man.

CHAPTER VII

THE MECHANISM OF CONSCIOUSNESS

1. THE DEVELOPMENT OF THE MECHANISM

IN a very real sense the whole of the bodies of man form the mechanism of consciousness, as organs for willing, thinking, and acting; but the nervous apparatus may be called its special mechanism, as that whereby, in the physical body, it controls and directs all. Every cell in the body is composed of myriads of tiny lives, each with its own germinal consciousness; [1] each cell has its own dawning consciousness, controlling and organizing these; but the central ruling consciousness which uses the whole body controls and organizes it in turn, and the mechanism in which it functions for this purpose is the nervous.

[1] The term "lives" signifies Units of Consciousness, but does not denote the kind of consciousness thus separated, nor necessarily imply the presence of a Jivatma. It means a cognizable "drop" from the ocean of consciousness, an atom or collection of atoms ensouled by consciousness and acting as a unit. An atom is a "life", the consciousness being that of the Third Logos. A microbe is a "life", the consciousness being that of the Second Logos, appropriated and modified, as before said, by the Planetary Logos and the Spirit of the Earth.

This nervous mechanism is the outcome of astral impulses, and consciousness must be active on the astral plane before it can be constructed.   Impulses set up by the consciousness—*willing* to experience and vaguely endeavouring to give effect to this Will—cause vibrations in etheric matter, and these vibrations, by the very nature of the matter,[1] become electric, magnetic, heat, and other energies. These are the masons which work under the impulse of the master-builder, Consciousness.   The impulse is from him; the execution is by them.   The directive intelligence, which as yet he cannot furnish, is supplied by the Logic life in the Group-Soul, and by the Nature-Spirits working under the guidance, as already said, of the Shining Ones of the Third Elemental Kingdom.

We have then to understand that nervous matter is built up on the physical plane under impulses from the astral, the directly constructive forces being indeed physical, but the guidance and the setting in motion of them being astral, *i.e.*, proceeding from consciousness active on the astral plane.   The life-energy, the prana, which flows in rosy waves, pulsing along the etheric matter in all nerves, not in their medullary sheaths but in their substance, comes down immediately from the astral plane; it is drawn

---

[1] The tanmatra and tattva of the plane, with its six sub-tan-matras and sub-tattvas.

from the great reservoir of life, the Logos, and is specialized on the astral plane and sent down thence into the nervous system, blending there with the magnetic, eletrical, and other currents which form the purely physical prana, drawn from the same reservoir, but through the Sun, His physical body; close examination shows that the constituents of the prana of the mineral kingdom are fewer and less complex in arrangement than those of the prana in the higher vegetable kingdom, and this again less so than that in the animal and human, and this difference is due to the fact that the astral prana mingles in the latter and not in the former—to any perceptible degree, at least. After the formation of the causal body, this complexity of the prana circulating in the nervous systems of the physical body increases much, and it appears to become yet more enriched in the progress of human evolution. For, as the consciousness becomes active on the mental plane, the prana of that plane mingles also with the lower, and so on as the activity of consciousness is carried on in higher regions.

We may pause a moment on this word " prana " that I have translated as " life-energy ". *Pran* is a Samskrit root, meaning to breathe, to live, to blow, made up of *an*, to breathe, move, live, and hence the Spirit, joined with the prefix *pra*, forth. Thus pra-an, pran, means to breathe forth, and life-breath, or life-energy, is the nearest English equivalent to the Samskrit term. As according to Hindu thought there is but one Life, one Consciousness, everywhere, the word Prana has been used for the Supreme Self, the all-sustaining Breath. It is the forth-giving energy of the One: for us, the Life of the Logos. Hence that Life on every plane may be spoken of as the Prana of the plane; it becomes the life-breath in every creature. On the physical plane it is energy, appearing in many forms, electricity, heat, light, magnetism, etc., transmutable into each other because fundamentally one; on other planes we have no names whereby to designate it, but the idea is definite enough. Appropriated by a being, it is prana in the narrower sense in which it is generally used in Theosophical literature, the individual's life-breath. It is the vital energy, the vital force, of which all other energies, chemical, electrical, and the rest, are merely derivatives and fractional parts; and it is a little quaint for the occultist when he hears scientific men talking glibly of chemical or electrical energy, and denouncing their parent, vital energy, as an " exploded superstition ". These partial manifestations of vital energy are merely due to the arrangements of matter in which it plays, cutting off one or another of its characteristics or perhaps all of them save one, as blue glass will shut off all the rays except the blue ones, and red all except the red.

In *The Secret Doctrine* H. P. Blavatsky speaks of the relation of prana to the nervous system. She quotes, and partly endorses, partly corrects, the view of " nervous ether", put forward by Dr. B. W. Richardson; the Sun-force is " the primal cause of all life on earth ", [1] and the Sun is " the storehouse of vital force, which is the noumenon of electricity ".[2] The " ' nervous ether ' is the lowest principle of the Primordial Essence which is Life. It is animal vitality diffused in all Nature and acting according to the condition it finds for its activity. It is not an ' animal product '; but the living animal, the living flower and plant, are its products." [3]

On the physical plane this prana, this life-force, builds up all minerals, and is the controlling agent in the chemico-physiological changes in protoplasm, which lead to differentiation and the building of the various tissues of the bodies of plants, animals, and men. They show its presence by the power of responding to stimuli, but for a time this power is not accompanied by distinct sentiency; consciousness has not unfolded enough to feel pleasure and pain.

---

[1] *Loc. cit.*, ii, 253, Fifth Adyar Edition.
[2] *Ibid.*, 255.
[3] *Ibid.*, 261.

When the current of prana from the astral plane, with its attribute of sentiency, blends with that of the prana of the physical plane, it begins the building of a new arrangement of matter—the nervous. This nervous arrangement is fundamentally a cell, details as to which can be studied in any modern text-book dealing with the subject,[1] and the development consists of internal changes and of outgrowths of the matter of the cell, these outgrowths becoming sheathed in medullary matter and then appearing as threads or fibres. Every nervous system, however elaborate, consists of cells and their outgrowths, these outgrowths becoming more numerous, and forming ever multiplying connections between the cells, as consciousness demands for its expression a more and more elaborated nervous system. This fundamental simplicity at the root of such complexity of details is found even in man, the possessor of the most highly evolved nervous organization. The many millions of neural ganglia [2] in the brain and body are all produced by the end of the third month of ante-natal life, and their development consists in expansion, and the outgrowth of their substance into fibres. This development in later life results from the activity of thought; as a man

---

[1] Such as Schäfer's "Histology" in Quain's *Anatomy*, tenth edition; Hallibutron's *Handbook of Psychology*, 1901; Wilson's *The Cell in Development and Inheritance*.

[2] Groups of nerve cells.

thinks strenuously and continuously, the thought-vibrations cause chemical activity, and the dendrons [1] shoot out from the cells, making connections and cross-connections in every direction, literal pathways along which prana pulsates—prana which is now composed of factors from the physical, astral, and mental planes—and thought-vibrations travel.

Returning from this digression into the human kingdom, let us see how the building of the nervous system, by vibratory impulses from the astral, begins and is carried on. We find a minute group of nerve cells and tiny processes connecting them. This is formed by the action of a centre which has previously appeared in the astral body—of which something will presently be said—an aggregation of astral matter arranged to form a centre for receiving and responding to impulses from outside. From that astral centre vibrations pass into the etheric body, causing little etheric whirlpools which draw into themselves particles of denser physical matter, forming at last a nerve cell, and groups of nerve cells. These physical centres, receiving vibrations from the outer world, send impulses back to the astral centres, increasing their vibrations; thus the physical and the astral centres act and react on each other, and each becomes more complicated

---

[1] Nerve processes, or prolongations, or outgrowths, consisting of the matter of the cell enclosed in a medullary sheath.

and more effective. As we pass up the animal kingdom, we find the physical nervous system constantly improving and becoming a more and more dominanat factor in the body, and this first-formed system becomes, in the vertebrates, the sympathetic system, controlling and energizing the vital organs —the heart, the lungs, the digestive tract; beside it slowly develops the cerebro-spinal system, closely connected in its lower workings with the sympathetic and becoming gradually more and more dominant, while it also becomes in its most important development the normal organ for the expression of the "waking-consciousness". The cerebro-spinal system is built up by impulses originating in the mental, not in the astral plane, and is only indirectly related to the astral through the sympathetic system, built up from the astral. We shall see later the bearing of this on the astral, sensitiveness of animals and lowly-developed human beings, the disappearance of this sensitiveness with the development of intellect, and its reappearance in the higher human evolution.

The permanent atoms form the imperfect but only direct channel between the consciousness manifesting as the spiritual Triad and the forms he is connected with. In the case of the higher animals these atoms are exceedingly active, and in the brief time between the physical lives considerable changes occur in these. As evolution goes on the increasing flow of life from the Group-Soul and through the permanent atom, as well as the increasing complexity of the physical apparatus, rapidly augment the sensitiveness of the animal. There is comparatively little sensitiveness in the lower animal lives, and little in fishes, despite their cerebro-spinal system. As evolution proceeds, the sense-centres continue to develop in the astral sheath, and in the higher animal these are well organized and the senses are acute. But with this acuteness there is brevity of sensations, and except with the highest animals little of the mental element mingles to lend increased and longer continued sensitiveness to sensation.

2. THE ASTRAL OR DESIRE BODY

The evolution of the astral body must be studied in relation to the physical, for while it plays the part of a creator on the physical plane, as we have seen, its own further development largely depends on the impulses received through the very organism it has created. It does not, for a long time, enjoy an independent life of its own on its own plane, and the organization of the astral body in relation to the physical is quite a different matter, and much earlier in time, than its organization in relation to the astral world. In the East they speak of the astral and mental vehicles of consciousness when acting in relation to the physical, as koshas, or sheaths, and use the term sharira, or body, for a form capable of independent action in the visible and invisible worlds. This distinction may serve us here.

The astral sheath of the mineral is a mere cloud of appropriated astral matter, and does not show any perceptible signs of organization. The same is the case with most vegetables, but in some there seem to be certain indications of aggregations and lines, which in the light of later evolution appear to be the dawn of incipient organization and in some old forest trees distinct aggregations of astral matter are visible at certain points. In animals these aggregations become clearly marked and definite, forming centres in the astral sheath of a permanent and specialized kind.

These aggregations in the astral sheath are the beginnings of the centres which will build up the necessary organs in the physical body, and are not the often-named chakras, or wheels, which belong to the organization of the astral body itself, and fit it for functioning on its own plane in connection with the mental sheath, as the lower type of the eastern sukshma sharira, or subtle body. The astral chakras are connected with the astral senses, so that a person in whom they are developed can

see, hear, etc., on the astral plane; they lie far ahead
of the point in evolution that we are considering, a
point at which the perceptive powers of consciousness have not yet any organ, even on the physical
plane.

As these aggregations in the astral sheath appear,
the impulses of consciousness on the astral plane,
guided as before explained, play on the etheric
double, forming the etheric whirlpools already
mentioned, and corresponding centres thus arise in
the astral sheath and physical body, the sympathetic
system being thus built up. This system always
remains thus directly connected with the astral
centres, even after the cerebro-spinal system is
evolved. But from the aggregations in the fore-
part of the astral sheath, ten important centres are
formed, which become connected with the brain
through the sympathetic system, and gradually
become the dominant organs for the activities of
the physical, or waking-consciousness—that is, for
that part of the consciousness which functions normally through the cerebro-spinal system. Five out
of the ten serve to receive special impressions from
the outside world, and are the centres through
which consciousness uses its perceptive powers;
they are called in Samskrit, Jnanendriyas, literally
" knowledge-senses " *i.e.*, senses, or sense-centres,
by which knowledge is obtained. These set up,

in the way before explained, five distinct etheric whirlpools, and thus construct five centres in the physical brain; these, in turn, severally shape and remain connected with their appropriate sense-organs. Thus arise the five sense-organs: the eyes, ears, tongue, nose, skin, specialized to receive impressions from the outer world, corresponding to the five perceptive powers of seeing, hearing, tasting, smelling, feeling. These are specialized ways in the lower worlds by which part of the perceptive ability of consciousness, its power of receiving external contacts, is exercised. They belong to the lower worlds and to the grosser forms of matter which shut consciousness in, and prevent it, thus enwrapped, from knowing other lives; they are openings in this dense veil of matter, permitting vibrations to enter in and reach the shrouded consciousness.

The remaining five of these ten astral centres serve to convey vibrations from consciousness to the outer world; they are the avenues outwards, as the knowledge-senses are the avenues inwards; they are named Karmendriyas, literally action-senses, senses or sense-centres which cause action. These develop like the others, forming etheric whirlpools which make the motor-centres in the physical brain; these, again, severally shape and remain connected with their appropriate motor-organs, hands, feet, larynx, and organs of generation and excretion.

We have now an organized astral sheath, and the continual action and reaction between this and the physical body improve both, and these together act on the consciousness and it reacts on them, both again gaining by this mutual interaction. And as we have already seen, these blind impulses of consciousness are guided in their play upon matter by the Logic life in the Group-Soul and by the Nature-Spirits. Always it is life, consciousness, seeking to realize itself in matter, and matter responding in virtue of its own inherent qualities, vitalized by the action of the Third Logos.

3. CORRESPONDENCE IN ROOT-RACES

A similar succession in the present, the fourth, Round marks the evolution of the kingdoms of Nature, the main characteristics of the previous Rounds being, as it were, repeated in the Root-Races, just as the history of evolution wrought out during long ages is repeated during the embryonic life of each new body. During the existence of the first two human Races there were conditions of temperature which would render sensibility destructive of any life-manifestation, and those Races show no sensibility to pleasure and pain on the physical plane. In the third Race there is sensibility to violent impacts, causing coarse pleasures and pains, but only some of the senses are evolved, those of hearing, touch, and sight, and these but to a low stage, as we shall presently see.

Now in the first two Races there are visible the beginnings of aggregations in the astral matter of the sheaths, and if these could connect themselves with appropriate physical matter there would be in the physical consciousness sensations of pleasure and pain. But the appropriate connections are lacking. The first Race shows a feeble sense of hearing, the second a vague response to impacts, the dawning sense of touch.

The spiritual Triad, at this stage of evolution, is so insensitive to vibrations from external matter that it is only when he receives the tremendous vibrations caused by impacts on the physical plane that he begins slowly to respond. Everything begins for him on the physical plane. He does not respond directly, but indirectly, through the mediation of the Logic life, and only as the primary physical apparatus is built up do the subtler impulses come through with sufficient force to cause pleasure and pain. The violent vibrations from the physical plane cause corresponding vibration on the astral, and he becomes dimly conscious of sensation.

CHAPTER VIII

FIRST HUMAN STEPS

1. THE THIRD LIFE-WAVE

THE middle of the third Root-Race had been reached; the nervous apparatus of animal man had been built up to a point at which it needed for its further improvement the more direct flow of thought from the spiritual Triad to which it was attached; the Group-Soul had completed its work for these, the higher products of evolution, as the medium by which the life of the Second Logos protected and nourished His infant children; it was now to form the foundation of the causal body, the vessel into which the downpouring life was to be received; the term of the ante-natal life of the Monad was touched, and the time was ripe for his birth into the lower world. The mother-life of the Logos had built for him the bodies in which he could now live as a separate entity in the world of forms, and he was to come into direct possession of his bodies and take up his human evolution.

We have seen that the Monads derive their being from the First Logos, and dwell on the anupadaka, the second, plane during the ages over which we have glanced. We have also seen that they appropriated to themselves with the help of different agents the three permanent atoms that represent them as Jivatmas on the third, fourth, and fifth planes, and also those which form the lower triad on the fifth, sixth, and seventh. All the communication of the Monad with the planes below his own has been through the Sutratma, the life-thread, on which the atoms are strung, that life-thread—of second plane matter—passing from the atmic atom to the buddhic, from the buddhic to the manasic, and from the manasic re-entering the atmic, thus making the " Triangle of Light " on the higher planes. We have seen further that from the line of this Triangle on the buddhic plane comes forth a thread, the Sutratma of the lower planes, on which the lower triad is strung.

The time has now come for a fuller communication than is represented by the delicate thread in its original form, and it, as it were, widens out. This is but a clumsy way of picturing the fact that the Ray from the Monad glows and increases, assuming more the form of a funnel: " The thread between the Silent Watcher and his shadow becomes more strong and radiant." [1] This downflow of monadic life is accompanied by much increased flow between

[1] *The Secret Doctrine*, i, 308, Fifth (Adyar) Edition.

the buddhic and manasic permanent atoms, and the latter seems to awaken, sending out thrills in every direction. Other manasic atoms and molecules gather round it, and a whirling vortex is seen on the three upper sub-planes of the mental plane. A similar whirling motion is seen in the cloudy mass surrounding the attached mental unit below, enveloped in the remaining layer of the Group-Soul, as already described. The layer is torn asunder, and caught up into the vortex above, where it is disintegrated, and the causal body is formed, a delicate filmy envelope, as the whirlpool subsides. This downflow of life, resulting in the formation of the causal body, is called the Third Life-Wave, and is properly ascribed to the First Logos, since the Monads came forth from Him and represent His triune life.

The causal body once formed, the spiritual Triad has a permanent vehicle for further evolution, and when Consciousness becomes able to function freely in this vehicle the Triad will be able to control and direct, far more effectively than ever before, the evolution of the lower vehicle.

The earlier efforts to control are not, however, of a very intelligent description, any more than the first movements of the body of the infant show they are directed by any intelligence, although we know that an intelligence is connected with it. The

Monad is now, in a very real sense, born on the physical plane, but still he must be regarded as a babe there, and must pass through an immense period of time before his power over the physical body will be anything but infantile.

2. HUMAN DEVELOPMENT

And this is clearly seen if we look at man as he was in his early days. Those long-perished Lemurians—if we except those entities who had already developed consciousness to a considerable extent, and who took birth in the clumsy Lemurian bodies in order to lead human evolution—were very poorly developed as to their sense-organs; those of smell and taste were not developed, but were only in process of building. Their sensitiveness to pleasure and pain was slight.

In the Atlanteans the senses were much more active; sight was very keen and hearing was acute; taste was more developed than among the Lemurians, but was still not highly evolved; coarse and rank foods were found perfectly tolerable and even agreeable, and very highly flavoured articles of diet, such as decaying meat, were preferred to more delicate viands, which were considered tasteless. The body was not very sensitive in injuries, and severe wounds did not cause much pain, nor were followed by prostration—even extensive lacerations failing to incapacitate the sufferer—and healing very quickly. The remnants of the Lemurian Race now existing, as well as the widely spread Atlantean, still show a relative insensitiveness to pain, and undergo, with very partial disablement, lacerations that would utterly prostrate a fifth Race man. A North American Indian has been reported as fighting on after the side of the thigh had been slashed away, and taking the field again after twelve or fifteen hours. This characteristic of the fourth Race body enables a savage to bear with composure, and to recover from, tortures that would prostrate a fifth Race man from nervous shock.

These differences derive largely from the varying developments of the permanent atom, the nucleus of the physical body. There is, in the fifth Root-Race, a fuller stream of life pouring down, causing greater internal development of the permanent atom, and increasing as that development proceeds. As evolution goes on, there is an increasing complexity of vibratory powers in the physical permanent atom, a similar increase in the astral atom, and again in the mental unit. As birth follows birth, and these permanent nuclei are put out on each plane to gather round them the new mental, astral and physical encasements, the more highly developed permanent atoms draw round them the more highly developed atoms on the planes to which they belong, and thus build up a better nervous apparatus through which the ever-increasing stream of consciousness can flow. In this way is built up the delicately organized nervous apparatus of the fifth Race man.

In the fifth Race man the internal differentiation of the nervous cells is much increased, and the inter-communications are much more numerous. Speaking generally, the consciousness of the fifth Race man is working on the astral plane, and is withdrawn from the physical body except so far as the cerebro-spinal nervous system is concerned. The control of the vital organs of the body is left to the sympathetic system, trained through long ages to perform this work, and now kept going by impulses from the astral centres other than the ten, without deliberate attention from the otherwise occupied consciousness, although of course sustained by it. It is, however, as we shall presently see, quite possible to draw the attention of consciousness again to this part of its mechanism, and to reassume intelligent control of it. In the more highly evolved members of the fifth Race, the main impulses of consciousness are sent down from the lower mental world, and work down through the astral to the physical, and there stimulate the physical nervous activity. This is the keen, subtle, intelligent consciousness, moved by ideas more than by sensations, and showing itself more actively in the mental and emotional brain-centres than in those concerned with sensory and motor phenomena.

The sense-organs of the fifth Race body are less active and acute than those of the highest fourth Race in responding to purely physical impacts. The eye, the ear, the touch do not respond to vibrations which would affect the fourth Race sense-organs. It is significant, also, that these organs are at their keenest in early childhood, and diminish in sensitiveness from about the sixth year onward. On the other hand, while less acute in receiving pure sense-impacts, they become more sensitive to sensations intermingled with emotions, and delicacies of colour and of sound, whether of nature or of art, appeal to them more effectively. The higher and more intricate organization of the sense-centres in the brain and in the astral body seems to bring about increased sensitiveness to beauty of colour, form, and sound, but diminished response to the sensations in which the emotions play no part.

The fifth Race body is also far more sensitive to shock than are the bodies of the fourth and third Races, being more dependent upon consciousness for its upkeep. A nervous shock is far more keenly felt, and entails far greater prostration. A severe mutilation is no longer a question merely of lacerated muscle, of torn tissues, but of dangerous nervous shock; the highly organized nervous system carries the message of distress to the brain-centres, and it is sent on from them to the astral body, disturbing and upsetting the astral consciousness. This is followed by disturbance on the mental plane; imagination is aroused, memory stimulates anticipation, and the rush of mental impulses intensifies and prolongs sensations. These again stimulate and excite the nervous system, and its undue excitation acts on the vital organs, causing organic disturbance; hence depression of vitality and slow recovery.

So also in the highly evolved fifth Race body, mental conditions largely rule the physical, and intense anxiety, mental suffering, and worry, producing nervous tension, readily disturb organic processes and bring about weakness or disease. Hence mental strength and serenity directly promote physical health, and when the consciousness is definitely established on the astral or the mental plane, emotional and mental disturbances are far more productive of ill-health than any privations inflicted on the physical body. The evolved fifth Race man lives physically literally in his nervous system.

3. Incongruous Souls and Bodies

But we should here notice a significant fact,
bearing on the all-important question of the relation
of the nervous organization to consciousness. When
a human consciousness has not yet grown beyond
the later Lemurian or earlier Atlantean type, but
is born into a fifth Race body, it presents a curious
and interesting study. (The reasons for such a
birth cannot here be enlarged upon; briefly, as the
more advanced nations annex the lands occupied by
little evolved tribes and kill them off either directly
or indirectly, the people thus summarily evicted
from their bodies have to find new habitats; the
suitable savage conditions are becoming rarer and
rarer, under the ever-expanding flood of higher
races, and they have to take birth under the lowest
available conditions, such as the slums of large
cities, in families of criminal types. They are
drawn to the conquering nation by karmic necessity.) Such persons incarnate in fifth Race bodies
of the worst available material. They then show
out in these fifth Race bodies the qualities that
belong to the earlier fourth or the third; and though
they have the physical outer nervous organization
they have not the internal differentiation in the
nervous matter that only comes with the play on
physical matter of energies coming from the astral

and mental worlds. We observe in them the non-responsiveness to impressions from outside, unless the impressions are of a violent order, that marks the low grade of development of the individual consciousness. We notice the falling back into inertia when a violent physical stimulus is absent; the recurrent craving for such violent stimulus when roused by physical necessities; the stirring into faint mental activity under vehement impact on the sense-organs, and the blankness when the sense-organs are at rest; the complete absence of any response to a thought or a high emotion—not a rejection but an unconsciousness of it. Excitement or violence in such a person is caused as a rule by something outside—by something coming before him physically which his dawning mind connects with the possibility of gratifying some passion, which he remembers and desires again to feel. Such a person may not be intent on robbery or murder at all, but may be stimulated into either or both by the mere sight of a well-dressed passer-by who seems likely to have money—money, that means gratification by food, drink, or sex. The stimulus to attack the passer-by is at once given, and will be followed at once by action, unless checked by a physical and obvious danger, such as the sight of a policeman. It is the embodied physical temptation which arouses the idea of committing the crime; a man who plans a crime beforehand is more highly developed; the mere savage commits a crime on the impulse of the moment, unless faced by another physical embodiment, that of a force which he fears. And when the crime is committed, he is impervious to all appeals to shame or remorse; he is susceptible only to terror.

These remarks do not, of course, apply to the intelligent criminal, but only to the congenital, brutal, and obtuse type, the third or fourth Race savage in a fifth Race body.

As the truths of the Ancient Wisdom more and more colour modern thought, they will inevitably, among other things, modify the treatment of the criminal. Such criminals as are here spoken of will not be punished brutally, but will be kept permanently under strict discipline, and will be, as far as is practicable, aided to progress more quickly than would have been possible under the conditions of savage life. But the further consideration of this would lead us too far from our main study, and we must now return to the workings of consciousness on the astral plane, as they show themselves in the higher animals and in the lower human types.

4. Dawn of Consciousness on the Astral Plane

We have seen that astral organization precedes and shapes the physical nervous system, and we have now to consider how this must affect the workings of consciousness. We should expect to find that consciousness on the astral plane will become aware of impacts on its astral sheath in a vague and unprecise way, just as, in the minerals and the plants and the lowest animals, it became aware of impacts on its physical body. This awareness of astral impacts will long precede any definite organization in the astral sheath, the bridge between the mental and the physical, that will gradually evolve it into an astral body, the independent vehicle of consciousness on the astral plane. And, as we have seen, the first organization in the astral sheath is a response to impacts received through the physical body, and is related to the physical body in its evolution. This organization has nothing to do directly with the reception, co-ordination, and understanding of astral impacts, but is engaged in being acted upon by, and re-acting on, the physical nervous system. Consciousness everywhere precedes Self-consciousness, and the evolution of consciousness on the astral plane proceeds contemporaneously with the evolution of Self-consciousness —to be dealt with presently—on the physical.

The impacts on the astral sheath from the astral plane produce vibratory waves over the whole astral sheath, and the ensheathed consciousness gradually becomes dimly aware of these surgings, without

relating them to any external cause. It is groping
after the much more violent physical impacts, and
such power of attention as it has evolved is turned
on them. The aggregations of astral matter, connected with the physical nervous systems, naturally
share in the general surgings of the astral sheath,
and the vibrations caused by these surgings mingle
with those coming from the physical body, and
affect also the vibrations sent down to it by the
consciousness through these aggregations. Thus a
connection is established between astral impacts
and the sympathetic system, and they play a considerable part in its evolution. As the consciousness
working in the physical body begins slowly to
recognize an external world, these impacts from
the astral—gradually classified under the five senses
as are the impacts from the physical—mingle with
those from the physical plane and are not distinguished as being different from them in origin.
This recognition is the lower clairvoyance, that
which precedes the great evolution of mind. So
long as the sympathetic system is acting as the
dominant apparatus of consciousness, so long will
the origin, astral or physical, of impacts remain as
the same to consciousness. Even the higher animals
—in whom the cerebro-spinal system is well developed, but in whom it is not yet, save in its sense-
centres, the chief mechanism of consciousness—fail

10

to distinguish between physical and astral sights, sounds, etc. A horse will leap over an astral body as though it were a physical one; a cat will rub herself against the legs of an astral figure; a dog will growl at a similar appearance. In the dog and the horse there is the dawning of an uneasy sense of some difference, shown by the fear of such appearances often manifested by the dog, and by the timidity of the horse. The nervousness of the horse—despite which he can be trained to face the dangers of a battle-field, and even, as with Arab mares, learn to pick up and carry away his fallen rider through all the alarming surroundings—seems chiefly due to his confusion and bewilderment as to his environment, and his inability to distinguish between what later he will learnedly call "objective realities", against which he can injure his body, and "delusions", or "hallucinations", through which his body can pass unscathed. To him they are all "real", and the difference of their behaviour alarms him; in the case of an exceptionally intelligent horse the nervousness is often greater, as he evolves a dawning sense of difference in the phenomena themselves, and this at first, not being understood, is yet more disquieting.

The savage, living more in the cerebro-spinal system, distinguishes between the physical and the astral phenomena, though the latter to him are as

" real " as the physical; he relates them to another
world, to which he relegates all things that do not
behave in the way he considers normal. He does
not know that, with regard to these, he is conscious
through the sympathetic and not through the
cerebro-spinal system; he is conscious of them—
that is all. The Lemurians and early Atlanteans
were almost more conscious astrally than they were
physically. Astral impacts, throwing the whole
astral sheath into waves, came through the sense-
centres of the astral to the sympathetic centres in
the physical body, and they were vividly aware of
them. Their lives were dominated by sensations
and passions more than by intellect, and the special
apparatus of the astral sheath, the sympathetic
system, was then the dominant mechanism of
consciousness.

As the cerebro-spinal system became elaborated,
and more and more assumed its peculiar position
as the chief apparatus of consciousness on the
physical plane, the attention of consciousness was
fixed more and more on the external physical world,
and its aspect of activity, as the concrete mind, was
brought into greater and greater prominence. The
sympathetic system became subordinate, and its
indications were less and less regarded, submerged
under the flood of the coarser and heavier physical
impacts from without. Hence a lessening of astral

consciousness and an increase of intelligence, though there still remains in almost every one a vague sense of non-understood impressions received from time to time.

At the present stage of evolution this lower form of clairvoyance is still found among human beings, but in persons of very limited intellect; they have little idea as to its rationale, and little control over its exercise. Attempts to increase it are apt to cause nervous disturbances of a very refractory kind, and these attempts are against the law of evolution, which works ever forward towards a higher end, and does not move backwards. As the law cannot be changed, attempts to work against it only cause disturbance and disease. We cannot revert to the condition in which the sympathetic system was dominant, save at the cost of health and of the higher intellectual evolution. Hence the serious danger of following many of the directions now published broadcast, to meditate on the solar plexus, and other sympathetic centres.

The practices, a few of which have come over to the West, are systematized into Hatha Yoga in India. Control over the involuntary muscles is regained, so that a man can reverse peristaltic action, inhibit the beating of the heart, vomit at will, and so on. Much time and trouble must be wasted ere the performance of such feats becomes possible, and at the end the man has only brought back to the control of the will muscles which have long since been handed over by it to the sympathetic system. As that handing-over was done by a gradual turning away of attention, so is it by a concentration of attention on the parts concerned that the earlier achievement is reversed. As such performances impose upon the ignorant, who regard them as evidences of spiritual greatness, they are often practised by men who desire power and are unable to obtain it in a more legitimate way. Moreover, they are the easiest form of Hatha Yoga, and are more easily cultivated, and cost far less suffering, than holding an arm extended till it withers, or lying on a bed of spikes.

When the cerebro-spinal system is thrown temporarily into abeyance, the impulses from the astral sheath through the sympathetic system make themselves felt in consciousness. Hence "lucidity" in trance, self-induced or imposed, the power of reading in the astral by the use of crystals, and other similar devices. The partial or complete suspension of the action of consciousness in the higher vehicle causes it to direct attention on the lower.

It may be well to add here, to prevent misconception, that the higher clairvoyance follows, instead of preceding, the growth of mind, and cannot appear until the organization of the astral *body*, in contra-distinction to the astral *sheath*, has been carried to a considerable height. When this is effected by the play of intellect and the perfecting of the physical intellectual apparatus, then the true astral senses before mentioned, called the chakras, or wheels, from their whirling appearance, are gradually evolved. These develop on the astral plane, as astral senses and organs, and are built and controlled from the mental plane, as were the brain-centres from the astral. Consciousness is then working on the mental plane and building its astral mechanism, as before it worked on the astral plane, building its physical mechanism. But now it works with far greater power and greater understanding, having unfolded so many of its powers. Further, its shape centres in the physical body from the sympathetic and cerebro-spinal system, to act as physical plane apparatus for bringing into the brain-consciousness the vibrations from the higher planes. As these centres are vivified, knowledge is "brought through," *i.e.*, is available for the use of consciousness working in the physical nervous system. This, as said, is the higher clairvoyance, the intelligent and self-directed exercise of the powers of the consciousness in the astral body.

In this upward-climbing, then, the powers of consciousness are awakened on the physical plane, and are then severally awakened on the astral and the mental. The astral and mental sheaths must be highly evolved ere they can be farther developed into the subtle body, acting independently on the higher planes, and then building for itself the necessary apparatus for the exercise of these higher powers in the physical world. And even here, when the apparatus is ready, built by pure thought and pure desire, it must be vivified on the physical plane by the fire of Kundalini, aroused and directed by the consciousness working in the physical brain.

CHAPTER IX

CONSCIOUSNESS
AND SELF-CONSCIOUSNESS

1. CONSCIOUSNESS

FOR an immense period of time—throughout the later vegetable and the animal evolution, and throughout the evolution of normal humanity up to the present time—the astral, or desire, sheath is, as we have seen, subordinate to the physical, so far as the workings of consciousness are concerned. We have now to trace the unfolding of the consciousness, of the life becoming aware of its surroundings. While the nervous system is truly said to be created *from* the astral plane, it is none the less created *for* the expression of consciousness on the physical plane, and for its effective working thereon. It is there that consciousness is first to become Self-consciousness.

When the vibrations of the outer world play on the physical sheath of the infolded infant Self, the Jivatma, the Ray of the Monad, they at first cause responsive thrills within that Self, a dawning consciousness within itself, a feeling unrelated by that Self to anything outside though caused by impacts from outside. It is a change outside the enveloping film of the Self, clothed in sheaths of denser matter, which outside change causes a change within that envelope, and this change causes an act of consciousness—consciousness of change, of a changed condition. It may be an attraction, a drawing towards, exerted by an external object over the sheaths, reaching to the envelope of the Self, causing a slight expansion in the envelope, following an expansion in the sheaths, towards the attractive object; and this expansion is a change of condition, and causes a feeling, an act of consciousness. Or it may be a repulsion, a driving away, again exerted by an external object against the sheaths, reaching to the envelope of the Self, causing a slight shrinking in the envelope, following the shrinking away of the sheaths from the repellent object; and this shrinking is also a change of condition and causes a corresponding change in consciousness.

When we examine the conditions of the enveloping sheaths under an attraction and a repulsion, we find they are entirely different. When the impact of an external object causes a rhythmical vibration in these envelopes—that is, when their materials are made to arrange themselves in undulating regular lines of rarefaction and densification—this arrangement of the enclosing matter permits an interchange of life between the two objects that have come into contact, and in proportion to the correspondence of the rarefactions and densifications in the two is the fullness of the interchange. This interchange, this partial union of two separated Lives through the separating sheaths of matter, is "pleasure", and the going out of the Lives towards each other is "attraction"; however complicated pleasure may become, herein lies its essence; it is a sense of "moreness", of increased, expanded life. The more fully developed the Life, the greater the pleasure in the realization of this moreness, in the expansion into the other Life, and each of the Lives thus uniting gains the moreness by union with the other. As rhythmical vibrations and corresponding rarefactions and densifications make this interchange of life possible, it is truly said that "harmonious vibrations are pleasurable". When, on the contrary, the impact of an external object causes a jangle of vibrations in the envelopes of the impacted object—that is, when the materials are made to arrange themselves irregularly, moving in conflicting directions, striking themselves against each other— the contained Life is shut in, isolated, its normal outflowing rays are checked, intercepted, even turned back on themselves. This check to normal action is "pain", increasing with the energy of the indriving, and the result of the driving-in process is "repulsion". Here, also, the more fully developed the Life, the greater the pain in this violent reversal of its normal action, and in the sense of frustration that accompanies the reversal. Hence, again, "inharmonious vibrations are painful". Be it observed that this is true of all the sheaths, although the astral sheath becomes specialized as the recipient of the class of sensations later called pleasurable and painful. Constantly, in the course of evolution, a general life-function thus becomes specialized, and a particular organ is normally used for its exercise. The astral body being the vehicle of desires, the need for its special susceptibility to pleasure and pain is obvious.

To return from this brief digression into the state of the envelopes to the germ of consciousness itself: we shall find it important to notice that there is herein no "awareness" of an external object, no such awareness as is ordinarily conveyed by the use of the word. Consciousness, as yet, knows nothing of an outer and an inner, of an object and a subject; the divine germ is now becoming conscious. It becomes consciousness with this *change* of conditions, with this movement in the sheaths, this expanding and contracting, for consciousness exists only in, and by, change. Here, then, for the separated divine germ is the birth of consciousness; it is born of change, of motion; where and when this first change occurs, there consciousness, for that separated germ, is born.

The mere clothing of this germ with successive envelopes of matter on successive planes gives rise to these first vague changes within the germ that are the birthing of consciousness; and none of us may count the ages which roll on as these changes become more defined, and as the envelopes become more definitely shaped by the ceaseless impacts from without, and the no less ceaseless responsive thrillings from within. The state of consciousness at this stage can only be described as one of "feeling", feeling becoming slowly more and more definite, and assuming two phases, pleasure and pain—pleasure with expansion, pain with contraction. And, be it noted, this primary state of consciousness does not manifest the three well-known aspects of Will, Wisdom, and Activity, even in the most germinal stage; "feeling" precedes these, and belongs to consciousness as a whole, though in later stages of evolution it shows itself so much in connection with the Will-Desire aspect as to become almost identified with it; in the plural, as feelings, indeed it belongs to that aspect, which is the first to arise as a differentiation within consciousness.

As the states of pleasure and pain become more definitely established in consciousness, they give rise to the three aspects; with the fading away of pleasure there is a continuance of the attraction in consciousness, a memory, and this becomes a dim groping after it, a vague following of the vanishing feeling, a movement—too indefinite to be called an effort—to hold it, to retain it; similarly with the fading away of pain there is a continuance of the repulsion in consciousness, again a memory, and this becomes an equally vague movement to push it away. These states give birth to: memory of past pleasure and pain, indicating the germination of the Thought-aspect; longing to experience again pleasure, or avoid pain, the germination of the Desire-aspect; this stimulating a movement, the germination of the Activity-aspect. Thus consciousness is differentiated into its three aspects from its primary unity of Feeling, repeating in miniature the kosmic process in which the triple Divinity ever arises from the One Existence. The Hermetic axiom is here, as always, exemplified: " As above, so below."

2.   SELF-CONSCIOUSNESS

Desire, thus germinated, gropes after pleasure, not, as yet, after the pleasure-giving object; for consciousness is as yet limited within its own kingdom, is conscious only in the within, is conscious only of changes in that within. It has not yet turned its attention outwards, is not yet conscious even that there is an outwards. Meanwhile that outwards of which it is not aware, is continually hammering at its vehicles, and most vehemently at its physical vehicle, the vehicle most easily affected from outside, and with most difficulty from within. Gradually the persistent and violent shocks from outside draw its attention in their direction; their irregularity, their unexpectedness, their constant assaults, their unrelatedness to its slow, groping movements, their unexplained appearances and disappearances are in opposition to its dim sense of regularity, continuity, of being always there, of slow surges of change rising and falling within what is not yet to it "himself"; there is a consciousness of *difference*, and this grows into a sense of a something that remains within a changing hurly-burly, a sense of a "within" and a "without", or, to speak more accurately, of a "without" and a "within", since it is the hammering outside that causes the difference of "without" and "within" to arise in consciousness. "Without" comes first, if only by a fraction of time, because its recognition alone makes possible and inevitable the recognition of "within". So long as there is nothing else, we cannot speak of "within"; it is everything. But when "without" forces itself on consciousness, "within" rises up as its inevitable opposite. This sense of a "without" arises necessarily at the points of contact between the continuing consciousness and the changing hurly-burly; that is, in its physical vehicle, its physical body. Herein is slowly established the awareness of "others", and with the establishment of this "others" comes the establishment also of "I" over against them. He becomes conscious of things outside instead of being conscious only of changes, and then he comes to know that the changes are in "himself", and that the things are outside himself. Self-consciousness is born.

This process of perceiving objects is a complex one. It must be remembered that objects contact the body in various ways, and the body receives some of their vibrations by the parts differentiated to receive such vibrations. The eye, the ear, the skin, the tongue, the nose, receive various vibratory waves, and certain cells in the organs affected vibrate similarly in response. The waves set up pass to the sense-centres in the brain, and thence to the knowl-edge-senses in the astral sheath; there the changes in consciousness take place which correspond with them, as explained in Chapter II, and they are sent on as these changes, the sensations of colour, outline, sound, form, taste, smell, etc., still as separate sen-sations, to consciousness working in the mental sheath, and are there combined by it into a single image, unified into a single perception of an object.

This blending of the various streams into one, this synthesis of sensations, is a speciality of the mind. Hence, in Indian psychology, the mind is often called " the sixth sense ", "the senses, of which mind is the sixth ".[1] When we consider the five organs of action in relation to the mind, we find a reverse process going on; the mind pictures a certain act as a whole, and thereby brings about a corresponding set of vibrations in the mental sheath; these vibrations are reproduced in the motor senses in the astral sheath; they break it up, analyse it into its constituent parts, and these are accompanied with vibrations in the matter of the motor centres; these, in turn, are repeated in the motor centres in the brain as separate waves; the motor centres distribute these waves through the nervous system to the various muscles that must co-operate to produce the action. Regarded in this double relation the mind becomes the eleventh sense, " the ten senses, and the one ".[2]

3.   REAL AND UNREAL

With the change of consciousness into Self-consciousness comes the recognition of a difference which later, in the more evolved Self-consciousness,

[1] *Bhagavad-Gita*, xv, 7.
[2] *Ibid.*, xiii, 5.

becomes the difference between the objective or
" real "—in the ordinary western sense of the word
—and the subjective or " unreal ", and " imagi-
nary ". To the jelly-fish, the sea-anemone, the
hydra, waves and currents, sunshine and blast, food
and sand touching the periphery or the tentacles,
are not " real ", are registered only as changes in
consciousness, as in truth they are also to the body
of the human infant; I say registered, not recognized,
since no mental observation, analysis, and judgment
are possible in the lower stage of evolution. These
creatures are not yet sufficiently conscious of
" others ", to be conscious of " themselves ", and
they only feel changes as occurring within the circle
of their own ill-defined consciousness. The external world grows into " reality " as the consciousness, separating itself from it, realizes its own
separateness, changes from a vague " am " into a
definite " I am ".

As this self-conscious " I " gradually gains in
clearness of self-identification, of separateness, and
distinguishes between changes within himself and
the impact of external objects, he is ready to take
the next step of relating the changes within himself
to the varying impacts from outside. Then follows
the development of Desire for pleasure into definite
desire for pleasure-giving objects, followed by
thoughts as to how to obtain them; these lead to

11

efforts to move after them when in sight, to search
for them when absent, and the consequent slow
evolution of the outer vehicle into a body well-
organized for movement, for pursuit, for capture.
The desire for the absent, the search, the success
or failure, all impress on the developing consciousness the difference between his desires and thoughts,
of which he is, or can be, always conscious, and the
external objects which come and go without any
reference to himself, and with disconcerting irre-
levance to his feelings. He distinguishes these as
" real ", as having an existence which he does not
control, and which affects him without any regard
to his likings or objections. And this sense of
" reality " is first established in the physical world,
as being the one in which these contacts between
the " others " and the " I " are first recognized by
consciousness. Self-consciousness begins its evolution in and through the physical body, and has its
earliest centre in the brain.

The normal man, at the present stage of evolution, still identifies himself with this brain-centre
of Self-consciousness, and is hence restricted to the
waking-consciousness, or consciousness working in
the cerebro-spinal system, knowing himself as " I ",
distinctly and consecutively, only on the physical
plane, that is, in the waking state. On this plane
he is definitely self-conscious, distinguishing between

himself and the outer world, between his own thoughts and outside appearances, without hesitation; hence on this plane, and on this plane only, external things are to him " real ", " objective ", " outside himself ".

On other planes, the astral and the mental, he is as yet conscious but not-self-conscious; he recognizes changes within himself, but does not yet distinguish between the self-initiated changes and those caused by impacts from without on his astral and mental vehicles. To him they are all alike, changes within himself. Hence all phenomena of consciousness occurring on super-physical planes—planes on which Self-consciousness is not yet definitely established—the normal, average man calls " unreal ", "subjective", "inside himself", just as the jelly-fish, if he were a philosopher, would designate the phenomena of the physical plane. He regards astral or mental phenomena as the result of his " imagination", *i.e.*, as forms of his own creating, and not as the results of impacts upon his astral or mental vehicle from external worlds, subtler indeed, but as " real " and " objective " as the external physical world. That is, he is not yet sufficiently evolved to have reached self-realization on those planes, and thus to have become capable of objectivizing there the external worlds. He is only conscious there of the changes in himself, the changes in consciousness, and the external world is consequently to him merely the play of his own desires and thoughts. He is, in fact, an infant on the astral and mental planes.

CHAPTER X

HUMAN STATES OF CONSCIOUSNESS

1. THE SUB-CONSCIOUSNESS

WE have already noticed the fact that many activities of consciousness, once purposive, have become automatic, and have gradually sunk below the " threshold of consciousness ". The processes which maintain the life of the body—such as the beating of the heart, the expansion and contraction of the heart, the processes of digestion, etc.—have all fallen into a region of consciousness on which the attention of consciousness is not fixed. And there are innumerable phenomena, not directly connected with the maintenance of bodily life, which also inhabit this dim region. The sympathetic system is a storehouse of traces left by long-past events—events not belonging to our present life at all, but events that passed hundreds of centuries ago, that occurred in long-past lives, when the Jivatma which is our Self was abiding in savage human bodies, and even in the bodies of animals. Many a causeless terror, many a midnight panic, many a surge of furious anger, many an impulse of vindictive cruelty, many a rush of passionate revenge, is flung up from the depths of that dark sea of the sub-conscious which rolls within us, concealing many a wreck, many a skeleton of our past. Handed down by the astral consciousness of the time to its physical instrument for putting into action, the ever-sensitive plate of the permanent atom has caught and photographed them, and has registered them in the recesses of the nervous system, life after life. The consciousness is off guard; or a strong vibration from another strikes us; or some event reproduces circumstances that start vibrations that arouse; in one way or another, the slumbering possibilities are awakened, and hurling itself upwards into the light of day comes the long-buried passion. There too hide the instincts which oft overpower reason, instincts that were once life-preserving efforts, or the results of experiences in which our body of the time perished, and the soul registered the result for future guidance. Instincts of love for the opposite sex, outcome of innumerable unions; instincts of paternal and maternal love, poured out in many generations; instincts of self-defence, developed in countless battles; instincts of taking undue advantage, off-spring of numberless cheatings and intrigues; and yet again there lurk there many vibrations that belong to events, and feelings, and desires, and thoughts of our present life, experienced and forgotten, but lying near the surface, ready for upcall. Time would fail to enumerate the contents of this relic-chamber of an immemorial past, containing old bones fit only for the dust-bin, side by side with interesting fragments of earlier days, with tools still useful for our present needs. Over the door of the relic-chamber is written: " Fragments of the Past". For the sub-consciousness belongs to the Past, as the waking-consciousness to the Present, as the super-consciousness to the Future.

Another part of the sub-consciousness in us is composed of the contents of all the consciousnesses that use our bodies as fields of evolution—atoms, molecules, cells of many grades. Some of the queer spectres and dainty figures that arise from the sub-conscious in us do not belong to us at all, but are the dim gropings, and foolish fears, and pretty fancies, of the units of consciousness at a lower stage of evolution than our own, that are our guests, inhabiting our body as a lodging-house.

In this part of the sub-conscious go on the wars, waged by one set of creatures in our blood against another set, which do not enter our consciousness, save when their results appear as diseases.

Human sub-consciousness, working on the physical plane, is thus composed of very varied elements, and it is necessary thus to analyse and to understand it, in order to distinguish its workings from those of the true human super-consciousness, which resembles the instincts in its sudden irruptions into consciousness, but differs entirely from them in its nature and place in evolution, belonging to the future while they belong to the past. These two differ as atrophied vestigial organs, recording the history of the past, differ from germinal rudimentary organs, indicating the progress of the future.

We have also seen that consciousness, working on the astral plane, built up and is still building the nervous system for its instrument on the physical plane; but this also does not form part of what is called the normal waking-consciousness at this stage of evolution. In the average man, consciousness, working on the mental plane, is now building up and organizing the astral body as its instrument in the future on the astral plane; but this again does not form part of the waking-consciousness. What then is the human waking-consciousness?

2. The Waking-Consciousness

The waking-consciousness is consciousness working on the mental plane and on the astral, using mental and astral matter as its vehicle, seated in the physical brain as Self-consciousness,[1] and using that brain with its connected nervous system as its instrument for willing, knowing, and acting on the physical plane. In waking-consciousness the brain is always active, always vibrating; its activity may be stimulated as a transmitting organ from outside through the senses, or it may be stimulated by the consciousness from the inner planes; but it is ceaselessly active, responding to the without and the within. In the average man, the brain is the only part in which consciousness has definitely become Self-consciousness, the only part in which he feels himself as " I ", and asserts himself as a separate individual unit. In all the rest of him consciousness is still vaguely groping about, answering to external impacts but not yet defining them, conscious as to changes in its own conditions, but not yet conscious of " others " and " myself ". In the more advanced members of the human family, consciousness, working on the astral and mental planes, is very rich and active, but its attention is not yet turned outwards to the astral and mental worlds in which it is living, and its activities find their outer expression in Self-consciousness on the physical

---

[1] See Chapter IX, §§ 1, 2, for the difference between consciousness and Self-consciousness; and Chapter VI, § 3, for the exposition of the physical consciousness, which must not be confused with waking-consciousness.

plane, to which all the outer attention in consciousness is turned, and into which is poured as much
of the higher working as it is capable of receiving.
From time to time, powerful impacts on the astral
or mental plane create so violent a vibration in
consciousness, that a wave of thought or emotion
surges outwards into the waking-consciousness and
throws it into such furious motion, that its normal
activities are swept away, submerged, and the man
is hurried into action which is not directed or
controlled by Self-consciousness. We shall consider
this further when we come to the super-physical
consciousness.

Waking-consciousness may, then, be defined as
that part of the total consciousness which is functioning in the brain and nervous system, and which
is definitely Self-conscious. We may conceive of
consciousness as symbolized by a great light, which
shines through a glass globe inserted in a ceiling,
illuminating the room below, while the light itself
fills the room above and sheds its radiance freely
in every direction. Consciousness is as a great egg
of light, of which only one end is inserted into the
brain, and that end is the waking-consciousness.
As consciousness becomes Self-consciousness on the
astral plane, and the brain develops sufficiently to
answer to its vibrations, astral consciousness will
become part of the waking-consciousness. Later

still, when consciousness becomes Self-consciousness on the mental plane, and the brain develops sufficiently to answer to its vibrations, the waking-consciousness will include mental consciousness. And so on, until all the consciousness on our five planes has evolved to waking-consciousness.

This enlarging of waking-consciousness is accompanied with development in the atoms of the brain, as well as with the development of certain organs in the brain, and of the connections between cells. For the inclusion of the astral Self-consciousness, it is necessary that the pituitary body should be evolved beyond its present condition, and that the fourth set of spirillæ in the atoms should be perfected. For the inclusion of the mental, the pineal gland must be rendered active, and the fifth set of spirillæ brought into thorough working order. So long as these physical developments remain unaccomplished, Self-consciousness may be evolved on the astral and mental planes, but it remains super-consciousness, and its workings do not express themselves through the brain and thus become part of the waking-consciousness.

Waking-consciousness is limited and conditioned by the brain so long as a man possesses a physical body, and any injury to the brain, any lesion, any disturbance, at once interferes with its manifestation. However highly developed may be a man's consciousness, he is limited by his brain so far as its manifestations on the physical plane are concerned, and if that brain be ill-formed or ill-developed, his waking-consciousness will be poor and restricted.

With the loss of the physical body, the connotation of waking-consciousness changes, and that which is here said of the physical conditions is transferred to the astral. We may therefore enlarge our original definition to the general statement: waking-consciousness is that part of the total consciousness which is working through its outermost vehicle, that is, which is manifesting on the lowest plane then touched by that consciousness.

In the earlier stages of human evolution, there is little activity in consciousness on the inner planes except as stimulated from the outer; but as Self-consciousness grows more vivid on the physical plane, it enriches with ever-increasing rapidity the content of consciousness on the inner; consciousness, working upon its content, rapidly evolves, until its internal powers far outstrip the possibilities of their manifestation through the brain, and the latter becomes a limitation and a hindrance instead of a feeder and a stimulator. Then the pressure of consciousness on its physical instrument becomes at times perilously great, causing a nervous tension which endangers the equilibrium of the brain, unable to adapt itself with sufficient rapidity to the powerful waves beating upon it. Hence the truth of the saying: " Great wits to madness near allied." Only the highly and delicately organized brain can enable the " great wits " to manifest themselves on the physical plane; but such a brain is the one most easily thrown off its balance by the strong waves of these same " great wits ", and this is " madness ". Madness—the incapacity of the brain to respond regularly to vibrations—may indeed be due to lack or arrest of development, lack or arrest of brain organization, and such madness is not allied to " great wits "; but it is a significant and pregnant fact that a brain in advance of normal evolution, developing new and delicately balanced combinations for the enriched expression of consciousness on the physical plane, is the brain of all others that may most easily be disabled by the throwing out of gear of some part of its mechanism not yet sufficiently established to resist a strain. To this again we must return in considering the super-physical consciousness.

3. THE SUPER-PHYSICAL CONSCIOUSNESS

Psychologists in the West have lately betaken themselves to the study of states of consciousness other than the waking; these are variously designated as " abnormal", " sub-conscious", " inconscient", and often as " dream-consciousness "—

because the dream is the most generally recognized
and universal form of other-consciousness. At first
there was a tendency to regard these states as the
result of disordered brain conditions, and this view
is still largely held; but the more advanced psychologists are outgrowing this narrow idea, and are
beginning to study such states as definite manifestations of consciousness under conditions not yet
understood, but not necessarily disorderly; some
definitely recognize a "larger consciousness", a
part only of which can find expression in the brain
as at present evolved. In the East, this state of
other-consciousness has for long ages been regarded
as higher than the waking state, as that of the consciousness set free from the narrow limits of the
physical brain, and acting in a subtler and more
plastic and congenial medium. Dream has been
regarded as one phase of this super-physical activity,
and as a touch with higher worlds; and means have
been taken to arouse Self-consciousness in the dream-
world, to set Self-consciousness, clothed in its higher
vestures, free from the physical body at will; so
that, instead of the vague and confused answers to
impacts from higher worlds in undeveloped dream
states, Self-consciousness may be established therein
with clear and definite vision. To effect this, Self-
consciousness in its higher vehicles must be at first
removed from the physical body and made active

on the astral plane; for until it knows itself out of the dense body, it cannot separate out in the " dream " the extra-physical experiences from the chaotic fragments of physical experiences mixed up with them in the brain. As clear water poured into a muddy bucket becomes mixed up with the mud, so does an astral experience, poured down into a brain full of fragments of past physical happenings, become blurred, confused, incongruous.[1] Eastern psychology hence sought after methods of separating the Self-consciousness from its physical vehicle, and it is interesting to observe that these methods, wholly different as they are from those used in the West, and directed to the intensifying of consciousness, reduce the body to the same state of quiescence as that induced by physical methods in the West, when the western psychologist betakes himself to the study of other-consciousness.

Super-consciousness includes the whole of the consciousness above the waking-consciousness; that is, all on the higher planes that does not express itself on the physical plane as Self-consciousness working through the brain. It is therefore a great complexity, and covers a large number of phenomena. Dream, as said, is part of it; so are all the workings of the astral consciousness asserting

[1] The student will do well to read carefully C. W. Leadbeater's useful book, *Dreams*.

themselves as premonitions, warnings, visions of happenings distant in space or time, vague touches from other worlds, sudden intuitions as regards character or events; also all the workings of the mental consciousness, lower or higher, that appear as intuitive grasp of truths, sudden insight into causal connections, inspirations—mental or moral—flashes of genius, visions of high artistic beauty, etc., etc. These irruptions of the super-consciousness into the physical plane have the character of unexpectedness, of conviction, of imperious authority, of lack of apparent cause. They are unrelated, or only indirectly related, to the contents of the waking-consciousness, and do not justify themselves to it but simply impose themselves on it.

To bring the super-consciousness into manifestation on the physical plane, it is necessary—in the early stages—to reduce the brain to inactivity, to render the sense-organs unresponsive to physical impacts, and, by expelling the conscious entity from the body, reduce that body to the state called trance. Trance is but the sleep-state, artificially or abnormally induced; whether produced by mesmeric, hypnotic, medicinal, or other means, the result is the same, so far as the physical body is concerned. But the result on the other planes will depend entirely on the evolution of consciousness on those planes, and a highly evolved consciousness would not permit the use of hypnotic or medicinal means—unless, perhaps, of an anæsthetic for an operation—though such a one might allow, under exceptional circumstances, the use of mesmerism in producing the trance state. Trance may also be produced by action from the higher planes, as by intense concentration of thought, or by rapt contemplation of an object of devotion, inducing ecstasy. These are the means used from time immemorial by the Raja Yogis of the East, and the ecstasy of the Saint in the West is produced by this rapt contemplation; the trance is indistinguishable from that produced by the means above referred to in the Salpetriere and elsewhere. The Hatha Yogis also reach this same trance condition, but by means much resembling the last named—by staring at a black spot on a white ground, at the point of the nose, and other similar practices.

But when other than physical vision and physical tests are used, how great is the difference between the super-physical conditions of consciousness in the hypnotized subject and in the Yogi! H. P. Blavatsky has well described this difference: " In the trance state the Aura changes entirely, the seven prismatic colours being no longer discernible. In sleep also they are not all ' at home '. For those which belong to the spiritual elements in the man, viz., yellow, Buddhi; indigo, Higher Manas; and the blue of the

12

Auric Envelope, will be either hardly discernible or altogether missing. The Spiritual Man is free during sleep, and though his physical memory may not become aware of it, lives, robed in his highest essence, in realms on other planes, in realms which are the land of reality, called dreams on our plane of illusion. A good clairvoyant, moreover, if he had an opportunity of seeing a Yogi in the trance state and a mesmerized subject side by side would learn an important lesson in Occultism. He would learn to know the difference between self-induced trance and a hypnotic state resulting from extraneous influence. In the Yogi, the ' principles ' of the lower quaternary disappear entirely. Neither red, green, red-violet, nor the auric blue of the body are to be seen; nothing but hardly perceptible vibrations of the golden-hued Prana principle, and a violet flame streaked with gold rushing upwards from the head, in the region where the Third Eye rests, and culminating in a point. If the student remembers that the true violet, or the extreme end of the spectrum, is no compound colour of red and blue, but a homogeneous colour with vibrations seven times more rapid than those of the red, and that the golden hue is the essence of the three yellow lines from orange-red to yellow-orange and yellow, he will understand the reason why; he (the Yogi) lives in his own Auric Body, now become the vehicle of Buddhi-Manas. On the other hand, in a subject in an artificially produced hypnotic or mesmeric trance, an effect of unconscious when not of conscious Black Magic unless produced by a high Adept, the whole set of the principles will be present with the Higher Manas paralyzed, Buddhi severed from it through that paralysis, and the red-violet Astral Body entirely subjected to the Lower Manas and Kama Rupa." [1]

This difference in the appearance of the entranced person, as seen by the clear-seeing eye, is connected with a difference of immense importance in the after outcome of the trance. The Yogi, who thus leaves the body, leaves it in full Self-consciousness, visits the higher worlds in full possession of his faculties, and, on returning to the dense body, imprints on the evolved brain the memory of his experiences. The little evolved person, entranced, "loses consciousness"; when his Self-consciousness is not developed on the higher planes, his awareness is not there turned outwards; he is practically as much asleep there, in the astral and mental worlds, as he is in the physical plane, and on awaking from the trance he knows nothing of what has occurred during its continuance, either here or elsewhere.

If, however, the subject be sufficiently evolved, as most people are at this stage of evolution, to be

[1] *The Secret Doctrine*, iv, 457, 458, Fifth (Adyar) Edition.

Self-conscious on the astral plane, then others may be profited by questioning him while entranced. For in the artificially induced trance state, wherein the brain is cut off from the normal action and reaction between itself and its environment, it becomes an instrument, however inadequate, of the super-physical consciousness. Isolated from its physical environment, rendered incapable of responding to its accustomed stimuli from outside, cut off from its lower attachments while remaining united to its higher, it continues to answer to the impacts from above, and can do this the more effectively since none of its energies are running out into the physical plane. This is the essence of the trance state. In the forcible closure of the avenues of the senses, through which its forces pour out into the external world, these forces remain available as servants of the super-physical consciousness. In the silence thus imposed on the physical plane, the voices of the other planes can make themselves heard.

In the hypnotic trance, a quickening of the mental faculties is observed: memory is found to embrace a far larger area, for the faint pulsings left by far-off events become audible when the stronger pulsings from the recent are temporarily stilled; people forgotten in the waking state are remembered in the trance; languages known in childhood, but since lost, reappear; trivial events re-arise. Sometimes the perceptive powers range over a larger area; distant occurrences are seen, vision pierces through physical barriers, far-off speech becomes audible. Fragments of other planes are also occasionally glimpsed, much mixed up with the thought-forms of waking hours. A whole literature exists on this subject, and can be studied by the investigator.

It has also been found that the results of deeper trance are not identical with those of the more superficial. As the trance deepens, higher strata of the super-physical consciousness manifest themselves in the brain. The famous case of Leonie I, II and III is well-known; and it should be observed that Leonie I knew nothing of Leonie II and III; that Leonie II knew Leonie I but did not know Leonie III; that Leonie III knew both Leonie I and II. That is, the higher knows the lower, while the lower does not know the higher—a most pregnant fact.

In the mesmeric trance, the higher phenomena are more easily obtained than in the hypnotic, and, in this, very clear statements may be had of the phenomena of the astral and even of the mental plane—where the "subject" is well developed— and sometimes glimpses are gained of past lives.

When we see that the exclusion of the physical plane is the condition for these manifestations of the super-physical consciousness, we begin to understand the rationale of the methods of Yoga practised in the East. When the methods are physical, as in Hatha Yoga, the ordinary hypnotic trance is most often obtained, and the subject on reawakening remembers nothing of his experiences. The method of the Raja Yoga, in which the consciousness is withdrawn from the brain by intense concentration, leads the student to continuity of consciousness on the succesive planes, and he remembers his super-physical experiences on his return to the waking state. Both in the West and in the East, the same cessation of waking-consciousness is aimed at, in order to obtain traces of the super-physical consciousness, or as the western psychologist would say, from the unconscious in man. The eastern method, however, with thousands of years of experience behind it, yields results incomparably greater in the realms of the super-physical consciousness, and establishes, on the sure basis of reiterated experiences, the independence of consciousness as regards its physical vehicle.

The ecstasy and the visions of Saints, in all ages and in all creeds, afford another example of the irruptions from the " unconscious ". In these, prolonged and absorbing prayer, or contemplation, is the means for producing the necessary brain-condition. The avenues of the senses become closed by the intensity of the inner concentration, and the same state is reached spasmodically and involuntarily which the practiser of Raja Yoga seeks deliberately to attain. Hence we find that devotees of all faiths ascribe their visions to the favour of the Deity worshipped, and not to the fact that they have produced in themselves a passive brain-condition, which enables the super-physical consciousness to imprint on that brain the sights and sounds of the higher worlds.

Prof. William James, in his *Varieties of Religious Experience*, points out that some of the most striking of these irruptions from the "unconscious" are cases of "sudden conversions", in which a sudden thought, or vision, or voice, has changed at once and completely the whole course of a man's waking life. He rightly argues that a force, sufficiently powerful to produce such effects, cannot be lightly waived aside or contemptuously ignored by any serious student of human consciousness. This whole class of psychical phenomena demands careful and scientific study, and promises a rich harvest of results, as to the super-physical consciousness, to repay the serious investigator.

As against this view, however, it is urged that these facts are observed in connection with morbid nervous states, and that the subjects are hysterical, over-excited persons, whose experiences are vitiated by their condition. In the first place, this is not always true; the eastern Raja Yogis are persons distinguished for their calmness and serenity, and some of the cases of conversion have been those of worldly and capable men.   Let it be granted, however, that in the majority of cases the nervous condition is morbid, and the brain over-strained, what then ? The normal brain is admittedly evolved to the point of responding to the vibrations of the physical world, and of transmitting these upwards, and of transmitting downwards mental and astral vibrations connected with these, from the higher vehicles.   It is not yet evolved to the point of receiving without disturbance very violent vibrations from the higher planes, nor of responding at all to the vibrations set up in the subtler vehicles by the external phenomena of their own planes.   Very violent emotions of joy, pain, grief, terror, often prove too much for the normal brain, causing severe headache, hysteria, and even nervous collapse.   It is, therefore, no wonder that the very violent emotion which causes what is called a conversion should often be accompanied by similar nervous distress. The important point is that when the nervous upset has passed, the effect—the changed attitude towards life—remains.   The nervous disturbance is due to the inadequacy of the physical brain to bear the violent and rapid vibrations dashing down upon it; the permanently changed attitude is due to the steady pressure of the super-physical consciousness continuously exerted. Where the super-physical consciousness is not sufficiently developed to exert this continuous pressure, the converted person "falls from grace" as the surge of emotion ebbs away.

In cases of visions and like phenomena, we have already seen that they may occur when a form of trance has been produced. But without this, such phenomena may occur in cases where the brain is in a state of tension, either from some temporary cause or from the fact that its evolution has gone beyond the normal. Strong emotion may increase the nervous tension to the point where response to direct astral vibrations becomes possible, and thus an astral happening becomes visible or audible. The reaction from the strain will probably show itself as nervous disturbance. When the brain is more highly evolved than the ordinary brain, has become more complicated and more sensitive, astral happenings may be felt constantly, and this strain may well be somewhat greater than the nervous system is quite fitted to bear, in addition to bearing the ordinary wear and tear of modern civilization. Hence, again, hysteria and other forms of nervous distress are likely to accompany the visions.

But these facts do not take away from the importance of the experiences, as facts in consciousness. Rather, perhaps, do they increase their importance, as showing the way in which evolution works in the action of the environment on an organism. The reiterated impacts of external forces stimulate the growing organism, and very often temporarily overstrain it; but the very strain forces forward its evolution. The crest of the evolutionary wave must always consist of abnormal organisms; the steady, normal, safe, average organisms follow on behind; they are most respectable, but perhaps not so interesting as the pioneers, and most certainly not so instructive as regards the future. As a matter of fact, the forces of the astral plane are constantly playing vigorously on the human brain, in order that it may develop as a fuller vehicle of consciousness, and a sensitive brain, in the transitional state, is apt to be thereby thrown a little out of gear with the world of its past. It is probable that a good many activities to which thought is at present directed will in the future be carried on automatically, and will gradually sink below the threshold of the waking-consciousness, as have done various functions once performed purposively.

As these changes go on, the subtler vibrations must inevitably show themselves in an increasing number in the most delicately equilibrated brains, those which are *not* normal, inasmuch as these—on the crest of evolution—will be those most capable of responding. Dr. Maudsley writes: " What right have we to believe Nature is under any obligation to do her work by means of complete minds only? She may find an incomplete mind a more suitable instrument for a particular purpose." [1] And Prof. James himself remarks: "If there were such a thing as inspiration from a higher realm, it might well be that the neurotic temperament would furnish the chief condition of the requisite receptivity." [2]

When we once recognize that forces subtler than the physical must necessitate for their expression a more refined vehicle than the brain organized for the reception of the physical, we shall cease to be troubled or distressed when we find that the superphysical forces often find their readiest expression through brains that are more or less out of gear with the physical plane. And we shall understand that the abnormal physical symptoms accompanying their manifestations in no way derogate from the value of these energies, nor from the importance of the part they will play in the future of humanity. At the same time the wish must naturally arise to find out some method whereby these forces may be enabled to manifest themselves without risking the destruction of their physical instrument.

[1] Quoted in Prof. James's book, mentioned above, p. 19. For " mind " read " brain ".

[2] *Ibid.*, p. 25.

This way has been found in the East in the practice of Raja Yoga, whereby the safe exercise of the higher consciousness is sought by intense concentration. This concentration, in itself, develops the brain as an instrument for the subtler forces, working in the brain-cells in the manner already described in connection with thought.[1] Moreover, it slowly opens up the set of spirillæ of the atom next in order to those now in activity, and thus adds a new organ for the higher functioning. This process is necessarily a slow one, but it is the only safe way of development; and, if its slowness be resented, it may be suggested as a reason for patience that the student is endeavouring to ante-date the atomic development of the next Round, and he can hardly expect to accomplish this with rapidity. It is, however, this slowness of the Raja Yogic practices which renders them somewhat unacceptable to the hurrying West; and yet there is no other way to secure a balanced development. The choice lies between this and the morbid nervous disturbances which accompany the irruptions of the super-physical consciousness into an unprepared vehicle. We cannot transcend the laws of Nature; we can only try to understand, and then to utilize them.

---

[1] See Chapter VII, § 1.

CHAPTER XI

THE MONAD AT WORK

1. BUILDING HIS VEHICLES

LET us now consider the work of the Monad in the shaping of his vehicles, when he has, as his representatives—as himself on the third, fourth, and fifth planes—Atma-Buddhi-Manas, with the causal body as the receptacle, the treasure-house, of the experiences of each incarnation.

At the close of each period of life, that is to say, at the end of each devachanic existence, he must stimulate into renewed activity the three successive nuclei of the bodies he is to wear during his next life-period. First, he arouses the mental nucleus. This arousing consists in increasing the flow of life through the spirillæ. It will be remembered that when the permanent units " went to sleep " the normal flow of life in the spirillæ lessened, and during the whole period of repose this flow is small and slow.[1] When the time for reincarnation arrives,

[1] See Chapter IV, §§ 4, 5.

this flow is increased, the spirillæ thrill with life, and the permanent units, one after another, behave as magnets, attracting round themselves appropriate matter. Thus when the mental unit is stimulated, it begins to vibrate strongly, according to the vibratory powers—the results of past experiences—stored up therein, drawing towards and arranging round itself appropriate matter from the mental plane. Just as a bar of soft iron becomes a magnet when a current is sent through a wire encircling it, and as matter within its magnetic field will at once arrange itself round that magnet, so is it with the permanent mental unit. When the life-current encircles it, it becomes a magnet, and matter within the field of its forces arranges itself round it and forms a new mental body. The matter attracted will be according to the complexity of the permanent unit. Not only will finer or coarser matter be attracted, but the matter must also vary in the development of the atoms which enter into the form-action of its aggregations. The molecules attracted will be composed of atoms the vibratory energies of which are identical with, or approach nearly to, or are in tune with, those of the attracting unit. Hence, according to the stage of evolution reached by the man, will be the development of the matter of his new mental vehicle. In this way, incarnation after incarnation, a suitable mental body is built up.

Exactly the same process is repeated on the astral plane in the building of the new astral body. The astral nucleus—the astral permanent atom—is similarly vivified, and acts in a similar way.

The man is thus clothed with new mental and astral bodies which express his stage of evolution and enable whatever powers and faculties he possesses to express themselves duly in their own worlds.

But when we come to the shaping of the body on the physical plane a new element appears. So far as the Monad is concerned, the work is the same. He vivifies the physical nucleus—the physical permanent atom—and it acts as a magnet like its fellows. But now it is as though a man interfered with the attraction and arrangement of matter within a magnetic field; the Elemental, charged with the duty of shaping the etheric double after the model given by the Lords of Karma, steps in and takes control of the work. The materials, indeed, may be gathered together, as a workman might carry bricks for the building of a house, but the builder takes the bricks, accepts or rejects, and sets them according to the plan of the architect.

The question arises: Why this difference? Why, on reaching the physical plane, where we might expect a repetition of the previous processes, should an alien power take the control of the building out of the hands of the owner of the house? The answer lies in the working of the law of karma. On the higher planes, the sheaths express as much of the man as is developed, and he is not there working out the results of his past relations with others. Each centre of consciousness, on those planes, is working within its own circle; its energies are directed towards its own vehicles, and only so much of them as is finally expressed through the physical vehicle acts directly upon others. These relations with others complicate his karma on the physical plane, and the particular physical form that he wears during a particular life-period must be suitable for the working out of this complicated karma. Hence the need for the adjusting interference of the Lords of Karma. Were he at a point of evolution at which he entered into similarly direct relations with others on other planes, similar limitations of his power to shape his vehicles on those planes would appear. In the sphere of his external activities, whatever it may be, these limitations must present themselves.

Hence the shaping of the physical body is done by an authority higher than his own; he must accept the conditions of race, nation, family, circumstances, demanded by his past activities. This limiting action of karma necessitates the building of a vehicle which is but a partial expression of the working

consciousness—partial, not only because of the
shutting off of power by the coarseness of the
material itself, but also because of the external
limitations above referred to. Much of his consciousness, even though ready for expression on the
physical plane, may thus be excluded, and only a
small part of it may appear on the physical plane
as waking-consciousness.

The next point in connection with this building
that we must consider is the special work of organizing the vehicles as expressions of consciousness,
leaving apart the general building by desire and
thought, with which we are so familiar. We are
concerned here with details, rather than with broad
outlines.

We know that while qualities are imparted to
matter during the descent of the Second Logos,
the arrangement of these specialized materials into
relatively permanent forms belongs to His ascent.
When the Monad, through his reflection as the
Spiritual Man, assumes some directive power over
his vehicles, he finds himself in possession of a form
in which the sympathetic nervous system is playing
a very large part, and in which the cerebro-spinal
has not yet assumed predominance. He will have
to work up a number of connecting links between
this sympathetic system which he inherits and the
centres which he must organize in his astral body,

13

for his future independent functioning therein. But before any independent functioning in any higher vehicle is possible, it is necessary to carry it to a fairly high point as a *transmitting vehicle*, that is a vehicle through which he works down to his body on the physical plane. We must distinguish between the primary work of the organization of the mental and astral vehicles that fits them to be transmitters of part of the consciousness of the Spiritual Man, and the later work of developing these same vehicles into independent bodies, in which the Spiritual Man will be able to function on their respective planes. Hence there are two tasks to be performed: first the organization of the mental and astral vehicles as transmitters of consciousness to the physical body; secondly, the organization of these vehicles into independent bodies, in which consciousness can function without the help of the physical body.

The astral and mental vehicles, then, must be organized in order that the Spiritual Man may use the physical brain and nervous system as his organ of consciousness on the physical plane. The impulse to such use comes from the physical world by impacts upon the various nerve-ends, causing waves of nervous energy to pass along the fibres to the brain; these waves pass from the dense brain to the etheric, thence to the astral, thence to the mental vehicle, arousing a response from the consciousness in the causal body on the mental plane. That consciousness thus roused by impacts from without, gives rise to vibrations, which flow down in answer from the causal body to the mental, from the mental to the astral, from the astral to the etheric and dense physical; the waves set up electric currents in the etheric brain, and these act on the dense matter of the nervous cells.

All these vibratory actions gradually organize the first inchoate clouds of astral and mental matter into vehicles which serve as effective fields for these constant actions and reactions. This process goes on during hundreds of births, started, as we have seen, from below, but gradually coming more and more under the control of the Spiritual Man; he begins to direct his activities by his memories of past sensations, and starts each activity under the impulse of these memories stimulated by desire. As the process continues, more and more forcible direction comes from within, and less and less directive power is exercised by the attractions and repulsions of external objects, and thus the control of the building up of the vehicle is largely withdrawn from the without and is centred in the within.

As the vehicle becomes more organized, certain aggregations of matter appear within it, at first cloudy and vague, then more and more definitely outlined. These are the future chakras, or wheels, the sense-centres of the astral body, as distinguished from the astral sense-centres connected with the sense-organs and centres of the physial body.[1] But nothing is done to vivify these slowly growing centres for immense periods of time, and the connection of them with the physical body is often delayed, even after they are functioning on the astral plane; for this connection can only be made from the physical vehicle, wherein the fiery force of Kundalini resides. Before Kundalini can reach them, so that they can pass their observations on to the physical body, they must be linked to the sympathetic nervous system, the large ganglionic cells in that system being the points of contact. When these links are made, the fiery current can flow through, and observations of astral events can be transmitted fully to the physical brain. While they can only be thus linked with the physical vehicle, the building of them as centres and the gradual organization of them into wheels can be begun from any vehicle, and will be begun in any individual from that vehicle which represents the special type of temperament to which he belongs. According as a man belongs to one typical temperament or another, so will be the place of the greatest activity in the building up of all the vehicles, in the gradual making of them into effective

[1] See Chapter VII, § 2.

instruments of consciousness to be expressed on the
physical plane. This centre of activity may be in
the physical, astral, lower, or higher mental body.
In any of these, or even higher still, according to
the temperamental type, this centre will be found
in the principle which marks out the temperamental
type, and from that it works " upwards " or " downwards," shaping the vehicles so as to make them
suitable for the expression of that temperament.

2. AN EVOLVING MAN

A special case may be taken to facilitate the
understanding of this process—a temperament in
which the concrete mind predominates. We will
trace the Spiritual Man through the third, fourth,
and fifth Root-Races. When we look at him at
work in the third Race, we find him very infantile
mentally, even though the mind is the predominant
note of his type. The surging life around him, that
he can neither understand nor master, works strongly upon him from outside and powerfully affects his
astral vehicle. This astral vehicle will be retentive
of impressions, in consequence of the temperament,
and the desires will stimulate the infantile mind to
efforts directed to their satisfaction. His physical
constitution differs from that of the fifth Race man;
the sympathetic system is still dominant, and the

cerebro-spinal system subordinate, but parts of the sympathetic system are beginning to lose much of their effectiveness as instruments of consciousness, belonging, as such instruments, to the stage below the human. There are two bodies in the brain especially connected with the sympathetic system in their inception, although now forming part of the cerebro-spinal—the pineal gland and the pituitary body. They illustrate the way in which a part of the body may function in one manner at an early stage, may then lose its special use and function little, if at all, and at a later stage of evolution may again be stimulated by a higher kind of life, which will give it a new use and function at a higher stage of evolution.

The development of these bodies belongs to the invertebrate rather than to the vertebrate kingdom, and the " third eye " is spoken of by biologists as the " invertebrate eye ". It is, however, still found as an eye among vertebrates, for a snake was lately found in Australia which showed on the top of the head a peculiar arrangement of semi-transparent scales; when these were cut away a complete eye was found underneath—an eye complete in its parts although not functioning. That third eye was functioning among the Lemurians in the vague and general way characteristic of the lower stages of evolution, and specially characteristic of the

sympathetic system. As our man advanced from the
Lemurian into the Atlantean Race, the third eye
ceased to function, the brain developed round it,
and it became the appendage now called the pineal
gland. As a Lemurian, he had been psychic, the
sympathetic system being largely affected by the
surgings of the undeveloped astral body. As an
Atlantean, he gradually lost his psychic powers, as
the sympathetic system became subordinate and the
cerebro-spinal grew stronger.

The growth of the cerebro-spinal system would be
more rapid in this Atlantean than in those of other
temperaments, because the main activity would be
in the concrete mind, and would thus stimulate and
fashion it; the astral body would lose its predominance sooner, and would become more rapidly a
transmitter of mental impulses to the brain. Hence,
when our man passed on into the fifth Race, he
would be peculiarly ready to take advantage of its
characteristic; he would build a large and well-
proportioned brain; he would utilize his astral
chiefly as a transmitter, and would build his chakras
from the mental plane.

3. THE PITUITARY BODY AND PINEAL GLAND

To return to the second of the two bodies mentioned above—the pituitary body. This is regarded
as developed from a primeval mouth, in direct

continuity with the alimentary canal of the inverte-
brates. It ceased to function as a mouth in the
vertebrates and became a rudimentary organ; but
it has retained a peculiar function in connection
with the growth of the body. It is active during the
normal period of physical growth, and the more
actively it functions, the greater the growth of the
body. In giants it has been found that this organ
is peculiarly active. Moreover, the pituitary body
sometimes again begins to function in later life,
when the bony framework of the body is set, and
then causes abnormal and monstrous growth at the
free points of the body, hands, feet, nose, etc., giving
rise to disfigurement of a most distressing kind.

As the cerebro-spinal system became dominant,
the earlier function of these two bodies disappeared;
but these organs have a future as well as a past.
The past was connected with the sympathetic system; the future is connected with the cerebro-spinal
system. As evolution goes on, and the chakras in
the astral body are vivified, the pituitary body
becomes the physical organ for astral, and later for
mental clairvoyance. Where too great a strain is
made upon the astral faculty of sight while in the
physical body, inflammation of the pituitary body
sometimes results. This organ is the one through
which the knowledge gained by astral vision is
transmitted to the brain; and it is also used in

vivifying the points of contact between the sympathetic system and the astral body, whereby a continuity of consciousness is established between the astral and physical planes.

The pineal gland becomes connected with one of the chakras in the astral body, and through that with the mental body, and serves as a physical organ for the transmission of thought from one brain to another. In thought-transmission the thought may be flashed from mind to mind, mental matter being used as the medium for transmission; or it may be sent down to the physical brain, and by means of the pineal gland may be sent, *via* the physical ether, to the pineal gland in another brain, and thus to the receiving consciousness.

While the centre of activity lies in the dominant principles of the man, the connection of the chakras with the physical body must be made, as said, from the physical plane. The object of this connection is not to make the astral vehicle a more efficient transmitter to the physical body of the energies of the Spiritual Man, but to enable the astral vehicle to be in full touch with the physical. There may be different centres of activity for the building up of transmitting vehicles, but it is necessary to start from the physical plane in order to bring the results of the activities of bodies functioning on other planes within the waking-consciousness. Hence the high importance of physical purity in diet and other matters.

People often ask: How does knowledge gained on higher planes reach the brain, and why is it not accompanied by a memory of the circumstances under which it was acquired? Anyone who practises meditation regularly knows that much knowledge that he has not gained by study on the physical plane appears in the brain. Whence comes it? It comes from the astral or mental plane, where it was acquired, and reaches the brain in the ordinary way above described; the consciousness has assimilated it on the mental plane directly, or it has reached it from the astral, and sends down thought-waves as usual. It may have been communicated by some entity on the higher plane, who has acted directly on the mental body. But the circumstances of the communication may not be remembered, for one of two reasons, or for both. Most people are not what is technically called " awake " on the astral and mental planes; that is, their faculties are turned inwards, are occupied with mental processes and emotions, and are not engaged in the observation of the external phenomena of those planes. They may be very receptive, and their astral and mental bodies may easily be thrown into vibration, and the vibration convey the knowledge which is thus given, but their attention is not turned to the person making the communication. As evolution goes on, people become more and more receptive on the astral and mental planes, but do not therefore become aware of their surroundings.

The other reason for the lack of memory is the absence of the connecting links with the sympathetic system before mentioned. A person may be "awake" on the astral plane and functioning actively thereon, and he may be vividly conscious of his surroundings. But if the connecting links between the astral and physical systems have not been made, or are not vivified, there is a break in consciousness. However vivid may be the consciousness on the astral plane, it cannot, until these links are functioning, bring through and impress on the physical brain the memory of astral experiences. In addition to these links, there must be the active functioning of the pituitary body, which focusses the astral vibrations much as a burning glass focusses the rays of the sun. A number of the astral vibrations are drawn together and made to fall on a particular point, and vibrations being thus set up in dense physical matter, the further propagation of these is easy. All this is necessary for "remembering".

4. The Paths of Consciousness

The question arises: Does consciousness always travel along the same path to reach its physical vehicle? Transits, we know, are sometimes made directly through the atomic sub-planes from plane to plane, and sometimes by passing through each sub-plane from the seventh to the first before reaching the atomic sub-plane next below. Which of these paths does consciousness follow? In its normal working, in the ordinary process of thinking, the wave comes steadily down through each successive sub-plane, from the mental through the seven astral sub-planes to the physical etheric, and so to the dense nervous matter. This wave sets up electrical currents in the etheric matter, and these affect the protoplasm of the grey cells. But when the peculiar flashes of consciousness occur, as in flashes of genius, or as in sudden illuminative ideas which flash into the mind—such a flash as comes to the scientific man when out of a great mass of facts there suddenly springs forth the unifying underlying law—then the consciousness pours downward through the atomic sub-planes only, and thus reaches the brain. This is the illuminative idea which justifies itself by its mere appearance, like the sunlight, and does not gain in compelling power by any process of reasoning. Thus reasoning comes to the brain by the successive sub-planes; authoritative illumination by the atomic sub-planes only.

CHAPTER XII

THE NATURE OF MEMORY

1. THE GREAT SELF AND THE LITTLE SELVES

WHAT is memory? And how does it work? By what means do we recover the past, whether near or remote? For, after all, whether the past be near or remote, belonging to this or to any anterior life, the means which govern its recovery must be similar, and we require a theory which will include all cases of memory, and at the same time will enable us to understand each particular case.

The first step towards obtaining a definite and intelligible theory is a comprehension of our own composition, of the Self with its sheaths, and their inter-relation; and we may here briefly restate the main facts in the foregoing chapters which directly bear on the problem of Memory. We must bear constantly in mind the facts that our consciousness is a unit, and that this unit of consciousness works through various sheaths, which impose upon it a false appearance of multiplicity. The innermost, or most tenuous, of these sheaths is inseparable from the unit of consciousness; in fact, it is this sheath which makes it a unit. This unit is the Monad, dwelling on the anupadaka plane; but for all practical purposes we may take it as the familiar Inner Man, the Tri-Atom, Atma-Buddhi-Manas, thought of as apart from the atmic, buddhic, and manasic sheaths. This unit of consciousness manifests through, abides in, sheaths belonging to the five planes of its activity, and we call it the Self working in its sheaths.

We must think, then, of a conscious Self dwelling in vehicles that vibrate. The vibrations of these vehicles correspond, on the side of matter, with the changes in consciousness on the side of the Self. We cannot accurately speak of vibrations of consciousness, because vibrations can only belong to the material side of things, the form side, and only loosely can we speak of a vibrating consciousness. We have changes in consciousness corresponding with vibrations in sheaths.

The question of the vehicles, or bodies, in which consciousness, the Self, is working, is all-important as regards Memory. The whole process of recovering more or less remote events is a question of picturing them in the particular sheath—of shaping part of the matter of the sheath into their likeness —in which consciousness is working at the time.

In the Self, as a fragment of the Universal Self—
which for our purpose we can take to be the Logos,
although in verity the Logos is but a portion of the
Universal Self—is present everything; for in the
Universal Self is present all which has taken place,
is taking place, and will take place in the universe;
all this, and an illimitable more, is present in the
Universal Consciousness. Let us think only of a
universe and its Logos. We speak of Him as
omnipresent and omniscient. Now, fundamentally,
that omnipresence and omniscience are in the individualized Self, as being one with the Logos, but
—we must put in here a but—with a difference;
the difference consisting in this, that while in the
separated Self as Self, apart from all vehicles, that
omnipresence and omniscience reside by virtue of
his unity with the One Self, the vehicles in which
he dwells have not yet learned to vibrate in answer
to his changes of consciousness as he turns his attention to one or another part of his contents. Hence
we say that all exists in him potentially, and not as
in the Logos actually; all the changes which go on
in the consciousness of the Logos are reproducible
in this separated Self, which is an indivisible part
of His life, but the vehicles are not yet ready as
media of manifestation. Because of the separation
of form, because of this closing in of the separate,
or individualized Self, these possibilities which are

within him as part of the Universal Self are latent, not manifest, are possibilities, not actualities. As in every atom which goes to the making up of a vehicle there are illimitable possibilities of vibration, so in every separated Self there are illimitable possibilities of changes of consciousness.

We do not find in the atom, at the beginning of a solar system, an illimitable variety of vibrations; but we learn that it possesses a capacity to acquire an illimitable variety of vibrations; it acquires these in the course of its evolution, as it responds continually to vibrations playing upon its surface; at the end of a solar system, an immense number of the atoms in it have reached the stage of evolution in which they can vibrate in answer to any vibration touching them that arises within the system; then, for that system, these atoms are said to be perfected. The same thing is true for the separated, or individualized, Selves. All the changes taking place in the consciousness of the Logos which are represented in that universe, and take shape as forms in that universe, all these are also within the perfected consciousness in that universe, and any of these changes can be reproduced in any one of them. Here is Memory: the reappearance, the reincarnation in matter, of anything that has been within that universe, and therefore ever *is*, in the consciousness of its Logos, and in the consciousnesses which

are parts of His consciousness. Although we think of
the Self as separate as regards all other Selves, we
must ever remember it is inseparate as regards the
One Self, the Logos. His Life is not shut out from any
part of His universe, and in Him we live and move and
have our being, open ever to Him, filled with His life.

As the Self puts on vehicle after vehicle of matter,
its powers of gaining knowledge become, with each
additional vehicle, more circumscribed but also
more definite. Arrived on the physical plane,
consciousness is narrowed down to the experiences
which can be received through the physical body,
and chiefly through those openings which we call
the sense-organs; these are avenues through which
knowledge can reach the imprisoned Self, though
we often speak of them as shutting out knowledge
when we think of the capacities of the subtler
vehicle. The physical body renders perception
definitive and clear, much as a screen with a minute
hole in it allows a picture of the outside world to
appear on a wall that would otherwise show a
blank surface; rays of light are truly shut off from
the wall, but, by that very shutting off, those allowed
to enter form a clearly defined picture.

2. Changes in the Vehicles and in Consciousness

Let us now see what happens as regards the
physical vehicle in the reception of an impression

14

and in the subsequent recall of that impression *i.e.*, in the memory of it.

A vibration from outside strikes on an organ of sense, and is transmitted to the appropriate centre in the brain. A group of cells in the brain vibrates, and that vibration leaves the cells in a state somewhat different from the one in which they were previous to its reception. The trace of that response is a possibility for the group of cells; it has once vibrated in a particular way, and it retains for the rest of its existence as a group of cells the possibility of again vibrating in that same way without again receiving a stimulus from the outside world. Each repetition of an identical vibration strengthens this possibility, each leaving its own trace, but many such repetitions will be required to establish a self-initiated repetition; the cells come nearer to this possibility of a self-initiated vibration by each repetition compelled from outside. But this vibration has not stopped with the physical cells; it has been transmitted inwards to the corresponding cell, or group of cells, in the subtler vehicles, and has ultimately produced a change in consciousness. This change, in its turn, reacts on the cells, and a repetition of the vibrations is initiated from within by the change in consciousness, and this repetition is a memory of the object which started the series of vibrations. The response of the cells to the vibration from outside, a response compelled by the laws of the physical universe, gives to the cells the power of responding to a similar impulse, though feebler, coming from within. A little power is exhausted in each moving of matter in a new vehicle, and hence a gradual diminution of the energy in the vibration. Less and less is exhausted as the cells repeat similar vibrations in response to new impacts from without, the cells answering more readily with each repetition.

Therein lies the value of the " without "; it wakes up in the matter, more easily than by any other way, the possibility of response, being more closely akin to the vehicles than the " within ".

The change caused in consciousness, also, leaves the consciousness more ready to repeat that change than it was first to yield to it, and each such change brings the consciousness nearer to the power to initiate a similar change. Looking back into the dawnings of consciousness, we see that the imprisoned Selves go through innumerable experiences before a Self-initiated change in consciousness occurs; but bearing this in mind, as a fact, we can leave these early stages, and study the workings of consciousness at a more advanced point. We must also remember that every impact, reaching the innermost sheath and giving rise to a change in consciousness, is followed by a reaction, the change in consciousness causing a new series of vibrations from within outwards; there is the going inwards to the Self, followed by the rippling outwards from the Self, the first due to the object and giving rise to what we call a perception, and the second due to the reaction of the Self, causing what we call a memory.

A number of sense-impressions, coming through sight, hearing, touch, taste and smell, run up from the physical vehicle through the astral to the mental. There they are co-ordinated into a complex unity, as a musical chord is composed of many notes. This is the special work of the mental body; it receives many streams and synthesizes them into one; it builds many impressions into a perception, a thought, a complex unity.

3.   MEMORIES

Let us try to catch this complex thing, after it has gone inwards and has caused a change in consciousness, an idea; the change it has caused gives rise to new vibrations in the vehicles, reproducing those it had caused on its inward way, and in each vehicle it reappears in a fainter form. It is not strong, vigorous, and vivid, as when its component parts flashed from the physical to the astral, and from the astral to the mental; it reappears in the mental in a fainter form, the copy of that which the mental sent inwards, but the vibrations feebler; as the Self receives from it a reaction—for the impact of a vibration on touching each vehicle must cause a reaction—that reaction is far feebler than the original action, and will therefore seem less " real " than that action; it makes a lesser change in consciousness, and that lessening represents inevitably a less " reality ".

So long as the consciousness is too little responsive to be aware of any impacts that do not come through with the impulsive vigour of the physical, it is literally more in touch with the physical than with any other sheath, and there will be no memories of ideas, but only memories of perceptions, *i.e.*, of pictures of outside objects, caused by vibrations of the nervous matter of the brain, reproducing themselves in the related astral and mental matter. These are literally pictures in the mental matter, as are the pictures on the retina of the eye. And the consciousness perceives these pictures, " sees " them, as we may truly say, since the seeing of the eye is only a limited expression of its perceptive power. As the consciousness draws a little away from the physical, turning attention more to the modifications in its inner sheaths, it sees these pictures reproduced in the brain from the astral sheath by its own reaction passing outwards, and there is the memory of sensations. The picture arises in the brain by the reaction of the change in consciousness, and is recognized there. This recognition implies that the consciousness has withdrawn largely from the physical to the astral vehicle, and is working therein. The human consciousness is thus working at the present time, and is, therefore, full of memories, these memories being reproductions in the physical brain of past pictures, caused by reactions from consciousness. In a lowly evolved human type, these pictures are pictures of past events in which the physical body was concerned, memories of hunger and thirst and of their gratification, of sexual pleasures, and so on, things in which the physical body took an active part. In a higher type, in which the consciousness is working more in the mental vehicle, the pictures in the astral body will draw more of its attention; these pictures are shaped in the astral body by the vibrations coming outwards from the mental, and are perceived as pictures by the consciousness as it withdraws itself more into the mental body as its immediate vehicle. As this process goes on, and the more awakened consciousness responds to vibrations initiated from outside on the astral plane by astral objects, these objects grow " real", and become distinguishable from the memories, the pictures in the astral body caused by the reactions from consciousness.

Let us note, in passing, that with the memory of an object goes hand in hand a picture of the renewal of the keener experience of the object by physical contact, and this we call anticipation; and the more complete the memory of an event the more complete is this anticipation. So that the memory will sometimes even cause in the physical body the reactions which normally accompany the contact with the external object, and we may savour in anticipation pleasures which are not within present reach of the body. Thus the anticipation of savoury food will cause " the mouth to water ". This fact will again appear when we reach the completion of our theory of Memory.

4. WHAT IS MEMORY?

Now, having noted the changes in the vehicles which arise from impacts from the external world, the response to these as changes of consciousness, the feebler vibrations produced in the vehicles by the reaction of consciousness, and the recognition of these again by consciousness as memories, let us come to the crux of the question: What is Memory? The breaking up of the bodies between death and reincarnation puts an end to their automatism, to their power of responding to vibrations similar to those already experienced; the responsive groups are disintegrated, and all that remains as a seed for future responses is stored within the permanent atoms; how feeble this is, as compared with the new automatisms imposed on the mass of the bodies by new experiences of the external, may be judged by the absence of any memory of past lives initiated in the vehicles themselves. In fact, all the permanent atoms can do is to answer more readily to vibrations of a kind similar to those previously experienced than to those that come to them for the first time. The memory of the cells, or of groups of cells, perishes at death, and cannot be said to be recoverable, as such. Where then is Memory preserved?

The brief answer is: Memory is not a faculty, and is not preserved; it does not inhere in consciousness as a capacity, nor is any memory of events stored up in the individual consciousness. Every event is a present fact in the universe-consciousness, in the consciousness of the Logos; everything that occurs in His universe, past, present, and future, is ever there in His all-embracing consciousness, in His " Eternal Now ". From the beginning of the universe to its ending, from its dawn to its sunset, all is there, ever-present, existent. In that ocean of ideas, all is; we, wandering in the ocean, touch fragments of its contents, and our response to the contact is our knowledge; having known, we can more readily again contact, and this repetition

—when falling short of the contact of the outside sheath of the moment with the fragments occupying its own plane—is Memory. All " memories " are recoverable, because all possibilities of image-producing vibrations are within the consciousness of the Logos, and we can share in that consciousness the more easily as we have previously shared more often similar vibrations; hence, the vibrations which have formed parts of our experience are more readily repeated by us than those we have never known, and here comes in the value of the permanent atoms; they thrill out again, on being stimulated, the vibrations previously performed, and out of all the possibilities of vibrations of the atoms and molecules of our bodies those sound out which answer to the note struck by the permanent atoms. The fact that we have been affected vibrationally and by changes of consciousness during the present life makes it easier for us to take out of the universal consciousness that of which we have already had experience in our own. Whether it be a memory in the present life, or one in a life long past, the method of recovery is the same. There is no memory save the ever-present consciousness of the Logos, in whom we literally live and move and have our being; and our memory is merely putting ourselves into touch with such parts of His consciousness as we have previously shared.

Hence, according to Pythagoras, all learning is remembrance, for it is the drawing from the consciousness of the Logos into that of the separated Self that which in our essential unity with Him is eternally ours. On the plane where the unity overpowers separateness, we share His consciousness of our universe; on the lower planes, where the separateness veils the unity, we are shut out therefrom by our unevolved vehicles. It is the lack of responsiveness in these which hinders us, for we can only know the planes through them. Therefore we cannot directly improve our memory; we can only improve our general receptivity and power to reproduce, by rendering our bodies more sensitive, while being careful not to go beyond their limit of elasticity. Also we can " pay attention "; *i.e.*, we can turn the awareness of consciousness, we can concentrate consciousness, on that special part of the consciousness of the Logos to which we desire to attune ourselves. We need not thus distress ourselves with calculations as to " how many angels can stand on the point of a needle", how we can preserve in a limited space the illimitable number of vibrations experienced in many lives; for the whole of the form-producing vibrations in the universe are ever-present, and are available to be drawn upon by any individual unit, and can be reached as, by evolution, such a one experiences ever more and more.

5. REMEMBERING AND FORGETTING

Let us apply this to an event in our past life: Some of the circumstances " remain in our memory", others are " forgotten ". Really, the event exists with all its surrounding circumstances, " remembered " and " forgotten " alike, in but one state, the memory of the Logos, the Universal Memory. Anyone who is able to place himself in touch with that memory can recover the whole circumstance as much as he can; *the events through which we have passed are not ours*, but form part of the contents of His consciousness; and our sense of property in them is only due to the fact that we have previously vibrated to them, and therefore vibrate again to them more readily than if we contacted them for the first time.

We may, however, contact them with different sheaths at different times, living as we do under time and space conditions which vary with each sheath. The part of the consciousness of the Logos that we move through in our physical bodies is far more restricted than that we move through in our astral and mental bodies, and the contacts through a well-organized body are far more vivid than those through a less-organized one. Moreover, it must be remembered that the restriction of area is due to our vehicles only; faced by the complete event, physical, astral, mental, spiritual, our consciousness of it is limited within the range of the vehicles able to respond to it. We feel ourselves *to be* among the circumstances which surround the grossest vehicle we are acting in, and which thus touch it from " outside "; whereas we " remember " the circumstances which we contact with the finer vehicles, these transmitting the vibrations to the grosser vehicle, which is thus touched from " within ".

The test of objectivity that we apply to circumstances " present " or " remembered " is that of the " common sense ". If others around us see as we see, hear as we hear, we regard the circumstances as objective; if they do not, if they are unconscious of that of which we are conscious, we regard the circumstances as subjective. But this test of objectivity is only valid for those who are active in the same sheaths; if one person is working in the physical body and another in the physical and the astral, the things objective to the man in the astral body cannot affect the man in the physical body, and he will declare them to be subjective halluci-nations. The " common sense " can only work in similar bodies; it will give similar results when all are in physical bodies, all in astral, or all in mental. For the " common sense " is merely the thought-forms of the Logos on each plane, conditioning each

embodied consciousness and enabling it to respond
by certain changes to certain vibrations in its
vehicles. It is by no means confined to the physical plane, but the average humanity at the present
stage of evolution has not sufficiently unfolded the
indwelling consciousness for them to exercise any
" common sense " on the astral and mental planes.
" Common sense " is an eloquent testimony to the
oneness of our indwelling lives; we see all things
around us on the physical plane in the same way,
because our apparently separate consciousness are
all really part of the One Consciousness ensouling
all forms. We all respond in the same general way,
according to the stage of our evolution, because we
share the same consciousness; and we are affected
similarly by the same things because the action and
reaction between them and ourselves is the inter-
play of the One Life in varied forms.

Recovery of anything by memory, then, is due
to the ever-existence of everything in the consciousness of the Logos, and He has imposed upon us the
limitations of time and space in order that we may,
by practice, be able to respond swiftly by changes
of consciousness to the vibrations caused in our
vehicles by vibrations coming from other vehicles
similarly ensouled by consciousness; thus only can we
gradually learn to distinguish precisely and clearly;
contacting things successively—that is, being in time

—and contacting them in relative directions in regard to ourselves and to each other—that is, being in space—we are gradually unfolded to the state in which we can recognize all simultaneously and each everywhere—that is, out of time and space.

As we pass through countless happenings in life, we find that we do not keep in touch with all through which we have passed; there is a very limited power of response in our physical vehicle, and hence numerous experiences drop out of its purview. In trance we can recover these, and they are said to emerge from the sub-conscious. Truly they remain ever unchanging in the Universal Consciousness, and as we pass by them we become aware of them, because the very limited light of our consciousness, shrouded in the physical vehicle, falls upon them, and they disappear as we pass on; but as the area covered by that same light shining through the astral vehicle is larger, they again appear when we are in trance—that is, in the astral vehicle, free from the physical; they have not come and gone and come back again, but the light of our consciousness in the physical vehicle had passed on, and so we saw them not, and the more extended light in the astral vehicle enables us to see them again. As Bhagavan Das has well said:

" If a spectator wandered unrestingly through the halls of a vast museum, a great art-gallery, at the dead of night with a single small lamp in one hand, each of the natural objects, the pictured scenes, the statues, the portraits, would be illumined by that lamp, in succession, for a single moment, while all the rest were in darkness, and after that single moment, would itself fall into darkness again. Let there now be not one but countless such spectators, as many in endless number as the objects of sight within the place, each spectator meandering in and out incessantly through the great crowd of all the others, each lamp bringing momentarily into light one object and for only that spectator who holds that lamp. This immense and unmoving building is the rock-bound ideation of the changeless Absolute. Each lamp-carrying spectator out of the countless crowd is one line of consciousness out of the pseudo-infinite lines of such, that make up the totality of the one universal consciousness. Each coming into light of each object is its potency, is an experience of the jiva; each falling into darkness is its lapse into the latent. From the standpoint of the objects themselves, or of the universal conscious-ness, there is no latency, nor potency. From that of the lines of consciousness, there is." [1]

As vehicle after vehicle comes into fuller working, the area of light extends, and the consciousness can turn its attention to any one part of the area and

[1] *The Science of Peace.*

observe closely the objects therein included. Thus, when the consciousness can function freely on the astral plane, and is aware of its surroundings there, it can see much that on the physical plane is " past " —or "future", if they be things to which in the " past " it has learned to respond. Things outside the area of light coming through the vehicle of the astral body will be within the area of that which streams from the subtler mental vehicle. When the causal body is the vehicle, the " memory of past lives " is recoverable, the causal body vibrating more readily to events to which it has before vibrated, and the light shining through it embracing a far larger area and illuminating scenes long " past " —those scenes being really no more past than the scenes of the present, but occupying a different spot in time and space. The lower vehicles, which have not previously vibrated to these events, cannot readily directly contact them and answer to them; that belongs to the causal body, the relatively per- manent vehicle. But when this body answers to them, the vibrations from it readily run downwards, and may be reproduced in the mental, astral, and physical bodies.

6. ATTENTION

The phrase is used above, as to consciousness, that " it can turn its attention to any one part of the area, and observe closely the objects therein included." This "turning of the attention" corresponds very closely in consciousness to what we should call focussing the eye in the physical body. If we watch the action taking place in the muscles of the eye when we look first at a near and then at a distant object, or *vice versa*, we shall be conscious of a slight movement, and this constriction or relaxation causes a slight compression or the reverse in the lenses of the eye. It is an automatic action now, quite instinctive, but it has only become so by practice; a baby does not focus his eye, nor judge distance. He grasps as readily at a candle on the other side of the room as at one within his reach, and only slowly learns to know what is beyond his reach. The effort to see clearly leads to the focussing of the eye, and presently it becomes automatic. The objects for which the eye is focussed are within the field of clear vision, and the rest are vaguely seen. So also, the consciousness is clearly aware of that to which its attention is turned; other things remain vague, "out of focus".

A man gradually learns to thus turn his attention to things long past, as we measure time. The causal body is put into touch with them, and the vibrations are then transmitted to the lower bodies. The presence of a more advanced student will help a less advanced, because when the astral body of

15

the former has been made to vibrate responsively to long past events, thus creating an astral picture of them, the astral body of the younger student can more readily reproduce these vibrations and thus also " see ". But even when a man has learned to put himself into touch with his past, and through his own with that of others connected with it, he will find it more difficult to turn his attention effectively to scenes with which he has had no connection; and when that is mastered, he will still find it difficult to put himself into touch with scenes outside the experiences of his recent past; for instance, if he wishes to visit the moon, and by his accustomed methods launches himself in that direction, he will find himself bombarded by a hail of unaccustomed vibrations to which he cannot instinctively respond, and will need to fall back on his inherent divine power to answer to anything which can affect his vehicles. If he seeks to go yet further, to another planetary system, he will find a barrier he cannot overleap, the Ring-Pass-Not of his own Planetary Logos.

7.   The One Consciousness

We thus begin to understand what is meant by the statement that people at a certain grade of evolution can reach this or that part of the kosmos;

they can put themselves into touch with the consciousness of the Logos outside the limitations
imposed by their material vehicles on the less
evolved. These vehicles, being composed of matter
modified by the action of the Planetary Logos of
the Chain to which they belong, cannot respond to
the vibrations of matter differently modified; and
the student must be able to use his atmic body
before he can contact the Universal Memory
beyond the limits of his own Chain.

Such is the theory of Memory which I present
for the consideration of Theosophical students. It
applies equally to the small memories and forgettings
of everyday life as to the vast reaches alluded to in
the above paragraph. For there is nothing small or
great to the Logos, and when we are performing
the smallest act of memory, we are as much putting
ourselves into touch with the omnipresence and
omniscience of the Logos, as when we are recalling
a far-off past. There is no " far-off ", and no
" near ". All are equally present at all times and
in all spaces; the difficulty is with our vehicles, and
not with that all-embracing changeless Life. All
becomes more and more intelligible and more peace-
giving as we think of that Consciousness, in which
is no " before " and no " after", no " past " and no
" future ". We begin to feel that these things are
but the illusions, the limitations, imposed upon us

by our own sheaths, necessary until our powers are evolved and at our service. We live unconsciously in this mighty Consciousness in which everything is eternally present, and we dimly feel that if we could live consciously in that Eternal there were peace. I know of nothing that can more give to the events of a life their true proportion than this idea of a Consciousness in which everything is present from the beginning, in which, indeed, there is no beginning and no ending. We learn that there is nothing terrible and nothing which is more than relatively sorrowful; and in that lesson is the beginning of a true peace, which in due course shall brighten into joy.

PART II

WILL, DESIRE, AND EMOTION

PART II

WILL, DESIRE, AND EMOTION

CHAPTER I

THE WILL TO LIVE

In the brief study of Origins which forms § § 1, 2 of the Introduction to this book, we saw that the Monad, coming forth from the First Logos, showed in his own nature the tri-unity of his Source, the aspects of Will, Wisdom, and Activity.

It is to the study of Will—showing itself as Will on the higher plane and as Desire on the lower—that we are now to turn our attention; and the study of Desire leads us to the study of Emotion, indissolubly attached to it. We have already seen that we are here because we have willed to live in the lower worlds, that the Will determines our stay here. But the nature and power and work of the Will are for the most part but little realized, for in the earlier stages of evolution it is not manifest on the lower planes save as Desire, and it must be studied as Desire before it can be understood as Will.

It is the Power-aspect of consciousness, ever veiled within the Self, hiding as it were behind Wisdom and Activity, but prompting both to manifestation. So hidden is its nature that many regard it as one with Activity, and refuse to it the dignity of an aspect of consciousness. Yet Activity is the action of the Self on the Not-Self, that which gives to the Not-Self its temporary Reality, that which creates; but Will hides ever within, impelling to Activity, attracting, repelling, the core of the Heart of Being.

Will is the Power which stands behind Cognition and stimulates Activity; Thought is the creative activity, but Will the motive power. Our bodies are as they are, because the Self has for countless ages set his Will that matter should be shaped into forms whereby he may cognize and energize on all outside himself. It is written in an ancient Scripture: "Of truth this body is mortal, O Maghvan, it is subject to death. Yet is it a resting-place of the immortal and bodiless Atma. . . . The eyes are intended as organs of observation for the Being, who dwelleth within the eyes. He who willeth, 'I shall smell', is the Atma, wishing to experience fragrance. He who willeth, 'I shall speak', is the Atma, wishing to utter words. He who willeth, 'I shall hear', is the Atma, wishing to listen to sounds. He who willeth, 'I shall think,' is the Atma. The mind is the celestial eye, observing all desirable objects. By means of the mental celestial eye, Atma enjoyeth all." [1]

[1] *Chhandogyopaniskat*, VIII, xii, 1, 4, 5.

This is the secret, the motive power, of evolution. True, the great Will traces the high road of evolution. True, spiritual Intelligences of many grades guide the evolving entities along that high road. But too little attention has been paid to the countless experiments, failures, successes, the little by-ways and twists and curls, due to the gropings of the separate Wills, each Will to Live trying to find Self-expression. The contacts from the outer world arouse in each Atma the Will to know what touches. He knows but little in the jelly-fish, but the Will to know shapes, in form after form, an ever-improving eye that hinders less his power of perception. As we study evolution, we become more and more conscious of Wills which shape matter, but shape it by groping experiments, not by clear vision. The presence of these many Wills makes the constant branching of the evolutionary tree. There is a real truth in Professor Clifford's playful story to the children about the great Saurians of an early age: "Some chose to fly and became birds; others chose to crawl and became reptiles." Often we see an attempt foiled, and then the attempt is made in another direction. Often we see the most clumsy contrivances side by side with the most exquisite adaptations. The latter are the results of Intelligences knowing their aims and constantly chiselling the matter into appropriate forms; the others are the outcome of the strivings from within, still blind and groping, but steadfastly set to Self-expression. If there were only outside designers, seeing the end from the beginning, Nature would present us with insoluble puzzles in her building, so many are the inadequate attempts, the ineffective designs. But when we realize the presence of the Will to Live in each form, seeking Self-expression, shaping his vehicles for his own purposes, then we can see alike the creative plan which underlies all—the plan of the Logos; the admirable adaptations which work out His plan—the labour of the building Intelligences; and the inapt contrivances and clumsy expedients—due to the efforts of the Selves that will, but have not yet the knowledge or the power to perform perfectly.

It is this groping, striving, struggling divine Self, which, as evolution goes on, becomes in ever-increasing measure the true Ruler, the inner Ruler, the Immortal. Anyone who grasps that he is himself that Immortal Ruler, seated within his Self-created vehicles of expression, gains a sense of dignity and power which grows ever stronger and more compelling on the lower nature. The knowledge of the truth makes us only free. The inner Ruler may still be hampered by the very forms he has shaped for self-expression, but knowing himself as the Ruler, he can work steadfastly to bring his realm into complete subjection. He knows that he has come into the world for a certain purpose, to make himself fit to be a co-worker with the Supreme Will, and he can do and suffer all which is necessary to that end. He knows himself divine, and that his Self-realization is only a question of time. Inwardly the divinity is felt, though outwardly it is not yet expressed, and there remains to become in manifestation what he is in essence. He is king *de jure*, not yet *de facto*.

As a Prince, born to a crown, patiently submits to the discipline which is fittting him to wear it, so the sovereign Will in us is evolving to the age when royal powers will pass into its grasp, and may patiently submit to the necessary discipline of life.

CHAPTER II

DESIRE

1. The Nature of Desire

When the Monad sends forth his rays into the matter of the third, fourth, and fifth planes, and appropriates to himself an atom of each of these planes,[1] he creates what is often called his "reflection in matter", the human "Spirit", and the Will-aspect of the Monad is mirrored in the human Atma, whose home is on the third or atmic plane. That first hypostasis is indeed lessened in powers by the veils of matter thus endued, but it is in no way distorted; as a well-made mirror produces a perfect image of an object, so is the human Spirit, Atma-Buddhi-Manas, a perfect image of the Monad, is, indeed, the Monad himself veiled in denser matter. But as a concave or convex mirror yields a distorted image of an object placed before it, so do the further reflections of the Spirit in, or involutions into, yet denser matter show but distorted images thereof.

[1] See Part I, Chapter IV, § 3.

Thus, when the Will, in its downward progress, veiling itself farther on each plane, reaches the world immediately above the physical, the astral world, it appears therein as Desire. Desire shows the energy, the concentration, the impelling characteristics of Will, but matter has wrenched away its control, its direction, from the Spirit, and has usurped dominion over it. Desire is Will discrowned, the captive, the slave of matter. It is no longer Self-determined, but is determined by the attractions around it.

This is the distinction between Will and Desire. The innermost nature of both is the same, for they are verily but one determination, the Self-determination of the Atma, the one motor-power of man, that which impels to Activity, to action on the external world, on the Not-Self. When the Self determines the activity, uninfluenced by attractions or repulsions towards surrounding objects, then Will is manifested. When outer attractions and repulsions determine the activity, and the man is drawn hither and thither by these, deaf to the voice of the Self, unconscious of the inner Ruler, then Desire is seen.

Desire is Will clothed in astral matter, in the matter which by the Second Life-Wave was formed into combinations, the reaction between which and consciousness would cause sensations in the latter.

Clothed in this matter, the vibrations of which are accompanied with sensations in consciousness, Will is modified into Desire. Its essential nature of giving motor-impulses, surrounded by matter which arouses sensations, answers by impelling energy, and this energy, aroused through and acting through astral matter, is Desire.

As in the higher nature Will is the impelling power, so in the lower nature desire is the impelling power. When it is feeble the whole nature is feeble in its reaction on the world. The effective force of a nature is measured by its Will-power or its Desire-power, according to the stage of evolution. There is a truth underlying the popular phrase, " The greater the sinner the greater the saint." The mediocre person can be neither greatly good nor greatly bad; there is not enough of him for more than petty virtues or petty vices. The strength of the Desire-nature in a man is the measure of his capacity for progress, the measure of the motor-energy whereby that man can press onwards along the way. The strength in a man that impels to reaction on his environment is the measure of his power to modify, to change, to conquer it. In the struggle with the Desire-nature which marks the higher evolution, the motor-energy is not to be destroyed but transferred; lower desires are to be transmuted into higher, energy is to be refined while losing nought of its power; and finally the Desire-nature is to vanish into Will, all the energies being gathered up and merged into the Will-aspect of the Spirit, the Power of the Self.

No aspirant, therefore, should be discouraged by the storming and raging of desires in him, any more than a horse-breaker is displeased with the rearings and plungings of the unbroken colt. The wildness of the young untrained creature, and his rebellion against all efforts to control and restrain, are the promise of his future usefulness when disciplined and trained. And even thus are the strainings of Desire against the curb imposed by the Intelligence, the promise of the future strength of Will, of the Power-aspect of the Self.

Rather does difficulty arise where desires are feeble, ere yet the Will has freed itself from the trammels of astral matter; for in such case the Will to Live is expressing itself but feebly, and there is little effective force available for evolution. There is some obstacle, some barrier, in the vehicles, checking the forthgoing energy of the Monad, and obstructing its free passage, and until that barrier is removed there is little progress to be hoped for. In the storm the ship drives onward, though there be peril of wreck, but in the dead calm she remains helpless and unmoving, answering neither to sail nor helm. And since in this voyage no final wreck is possible, but only temporary damage, and the storm works for progress rather than the calm, those who find themselves storm-tossed may look forward with sure conviction to the day when the storm-gusts of Desire will be changed into the steady wind of Will.

2. THE AWAKENING OF DESIRE

To the astral world we refer all our sensations. The centres by which we feel lie in the astral body, and the reactions of these to contacts give rise to feelings of pleasure and pain in consciousness. The ordinary physiologist traces sensation of pleasure and pain from the point of contact to the brain-centre, recognizing only nervous vibrations between periphery and centre, and in the centre the reaction of consciousness as sensation. We follow the vibrations further, finding only vibrations in the brain-centre and in the ether permeating it, and seeing in the astral centre the point at which the reaction of consciousness takes place. When a dislocation between the physical and astral bodies occurs, whether by the action of chloroform, ether, laughing gas, or other drugs, the physical body, despite all its nervous apparatus, feels no more than if bereft of nerves. The links between the physical body and the body of sensation are thrown out of gear, and consciousness does not respond to any stimulus applied.

The awakening of Desire takes place in this body of sensation, and follows the first dim sensings of pleasure and pain. As before pointed out [1] pleasure " is a sense of ' moreness ', of increased, expanded life", while pain is a shutting in or lessening of life, and these belong to the whole consciousness. " This primary state of consciousness does not manifest the three well-known aspects of Will, Wisdom, and Activity, even in the most germinal stage; ' feeling ' precedes these, and belongs to consciousness as a whole, though in later stages of evolution it shows itself so much in connection with the Will-Desire aspect as to become almost identified with it." " As the states of pleasure and pain become more definitely established in consciousness they give rise to another; with the fading away of pleasure there is a continuation of the attraction in consciousness, and this becomes a dim groping after it "—a groping, be it noted, not after any pleasure-giving object, but after a continuance of the feeling of pleasure—" a vague following of the vanishing feeling, a movement—too indefinite to be called an effort—to hold it, to retain it; similarly with the fading away of pain there is a continuation of the repulsion in consciousness. . . . and this

[1] See Part I, Chapter IX, 1.

16

becomes an equally vague movement to push it away." These stages give birth to Desire.

This arising of Desire is a feeble reaching out of the life in search of pleasure, a movement of the life, undirected, vague, groping. Beyond this it cannot go, until Thought has developed to a certain extent, and has recognized an outer world, a Not-Self, and has learned to relate various objects in the Not-Self to the pleasure or pain arising in consciousness on contracting them.

But the results of these contacts, long before the objects are recognized, have caused, as above indicated, a division in, a forking of, Desire. We may take as one of the simplest illustrations the craving for food in a lowly organism; as the physical body wastes, becomes less, a sense of pain arises in the astral body, a want, a craving, vague and indeterminate; the body, by its wasting, has become a less effective vehicle of the life pouring down through the astral, and this check causes pain. A current in the water that bathes the organism brings food up against the body; it is absorbed, the waste is repaired, the life flows on unobstructed; there is pleasure. At a little higher stage, when pain arises, there is the desire to escape from it, the sense of repulsion arises, the contrary to the sense of attraction, caused by pleasure. There results from this that Desire is cloven in twain. From the Will to Live arose the longing to experience, and in the lower vehicle this longing, appearing as Desire, becomes on the one hand a longing for experiences that make the feeling of life more vivid, and on the other a shrinking from all that weakens and depresses. This attraction and repulsion are equally of the nature of Desire. Just as a magnet attracts or repels certain metals, so does the embodied Self attract and repel. Both attraction and repulsion are Desire, and these are the two great motor-energies in life, into which all desires are ultimately resolvable. The Self comes under the bondage of Desire, of Attraction-Repulsion, and is attracted hither and thither, repelled from this or that, hurried about among pleasure and pain-giving objects, as a helmless ship amid the currents of air and sea.

3. THE RELATION OF DESIRE TO THOUGHT

We have now to consider the relation that Desire bears to Thought, and see how it first rules and then is ruled by the latter.

The Pure Reason is the reflection of the Wisdom-aspect of the Monad, and appears in the human Spirit as Buddhi. But it is not the relation of Desire to the Pure Reason with which we are concerned, for it cannot, in fact, be said to be directly

related to Wisdom, but to Love, the manifestation
of Wisdom on the astral plane. We are to seek
rather its relation to the Activity-aspect of the
Monad, showing itself on the astral plane as sensation and on the mental as thought. Nor are we
even concerned with the Higher Mind, which is
creative Activity, Manas, in its purity; but with the
distorted reflection of this, the lower mind. It is
this lower mind which is immediately related to
Desire, and is inextricably intermingled with it in
human evolution; so closely joined, indeed, are
they, that we often speak of Kama-Manas, Desire-
Mind, as of a single thing, so rare is it, in the lower
consciousness, to find a single thought which is
uninfluenced by a desire. " Manas verily is declared to be twofold, pure and impure; the impure
is determined by desire, the pure is desire-
free." [1]

This lower mind is " thought " on the mental
plane; its characteristic property is that it asserts
and denies; it knows by difference; it perceives,
and remembers. On the astral plane, as we have
seen, the same aspect that on the mental plane is
thought appears as sensation, and is aroused by
contact with the external world.

When a pleasure has been experienced, and has
passed away, Desire arises to experience it again,

[1] *Bindopanishad*, 1.

as we have seen. And this fact implies *memory*, which is a function of the mind. Here, as ever, are we reminded that consciousness is ever acting in its threefold nature, though one or other aspect may predominate, for even the most germinal desire cannot arise without memory being present. The sensation caused by an external impact must have been many times aroused, before the mind will establish a relation between the sensation of which it is conscious and the external object which has caused the sensation. At last the mind " perceives " the object, *i.e.*, relates it to one of its own changes, recognizes a modification in itself caused by the external object. Repetitions of this perception will establish a definite link in memory between the object and the pleasurable or painful sensation, and when Desire presses for the repetition of pleasure, the mind recalls the object which supplied that pleasure. Thus the mingling of Thought with Desire gives birth to a particular desire, to find and appropriate the pleasure-giving object.

This desire impels the mind to exert its inherent activity. Discomfort being caused by the unsatis-fied craving, effort is made to escape the discomfort by supplying the object wanted. The mind plans, schemes, drives the body into action, in order to satisfy the cravings of Desire. And similarly, equally prompted by Desire, the mind plans, schemes, drives the body into action in order to avoid the recurrence of pain from an object recognized as pain-giving.

Such is the relation of Desire to Thought. It rouses, stimulates, urges on, mental efforts. The mind is, in its early stages, the slave of Desire, and the rapidity of its growth is in proportion to the fierce urgings of Desire. We desire, and thus are forced to think.

4.   Desire, Thought, Action

The third stage of the contact of the Self with the Not-Self is Action. The mind having perceived the object of desire, leads to, guides, and shapes the action. Action is often said to arise from Desire, but Desire alone could only arouse movement, or chaotic action. The force of Desire is propulsive, not directive. Thought it is that adds the element of direction, and shapes the action purposively.

This is the ever-recurring cycle in consciousness —Desire, Thought, Action. The propulsive power of Desire arouses Thought; the directive power of Thought guides Action. This sequence is invariable, and the clear understanding thereof is of the profoundest importance, for the effective control of conduct depends on this understanding and on its application in practice. The shaping of karma can only be achieved when this sequence is understood, for evitable and inevitable action can only thus be discriminated.

It is by Thought that we can change Desire, and thereby change Action. When the mind sees that certain desires have impelled to thoughts that have directed actions which were productive of unhappiness, it can resist the future promptings of Desire in a similar direction, and refuse to guide actions to a result already known as disastrous. It can picture the painful results, and thus arouse the repellent energy of Desire, and can image the blissful outcome of desires of the opposite kind. The creative activity of Thought can be exerted in the moulding of Desire, and its propulsive energy can be turned into a better direction. In this way Thought can be used to master Desire, and it may become the ruler instead of the slave. And as it thus asserts control over its unruly companion, it begins the transmutation of Desire into Will, changing the governance of the outgoing energy from the outer to the inner, from the external objects that attract or repel to the Spirit, the inner Ruler.

5. THE BINDING NATURE OF DESIRE

Since the Will to Live is the cause of the forthgoing, of the life seeking embodiment and appropriating to itself that which is necessary for its manifestation and persistence in form, Desire, being Will on a lower plane, will show similar characteristics, seeking to appropriate, to draw into itself, to make part of itself that whereby its life in form may be maintained and strengthened. When we desire an object, we seek to make it part of ourselves, part of the " I ", so that it may form part of the embodiment of the " I ". Desire is the putting forth of the power of attraction; it draws the desired object to itself. Whatever we desire, we attach to ourselves. By the desire to possess it, a bond is established between the object and the desirer. We tie to the Self this portion of the Not-Self, and the bond exists until the object is possessed, or until the Self has broken off the bond and repudiated the object. These are " the bonds of the heart ", [1] and tie the Self to the wheel of births and deaths.

These bonds between the desirer and the objects of desire are like ropes that draw the Self to the place where the objects of desire are found, and thus determine its birth into one or another world. On this runs the verse: " He also who is attached ever obtains by action that on which his mind has set its mark. Having obtained the object of action he here performs, he comes again therefore from that

[1] *Kathopanishad*, vi, 15.

world to this world for the sake of action. Thus is it with the desiring mind." [1] If a man desires the objects of another world more than the objects of this, then into that world will he be born. There is a continuing tension in the bond of Desire until the Self and the object are united.

The one great determining energy, the Will to Live, which holds the planets in their paths around the sun, which prevents the matter of the globes from scattering, which holds our own bodies together, that is the energy of Desire. That which rules all is in us as Desire, and it must draw to us, or draw us to, everything into which it has fixed its hooks. The hook of Desire fixes itself in an object, as a harpoon in the whale at which it is flung by the harpooner. When Desire has fixed its harpoon in an object, the Self is attached to that object, has appropriated it in Will, and presently must appropriate it in action. Hence a great Teacher has said: "If thy right eye offend thee, pluck it out and cast it from thee . . . if thy right hand offend thee, cut it off and cast it from thee." [2] The thing desired becomes part of the body of the Self, and if it be evil it should be torn out, at whatever cost of anguish. Otherwise it will only be worn a way by the slow attribution of time and of weariness.

[1] *Brihadaranyakopanishad*, IV, iv, 6.
[2] *Matt.*, v, 29, 30.

" Only the strong can kill it out. The weak must wait for its growth, its fruition, its death." [1]

6. The Breaking of the Bonds

For the breaking of the bonds of Desires, recourse must be had to the mind.   Therein lies the power which shall first purify and then transmute Desire.

The mind records the results which follow the appropriation of each object of Desire, and marks whether happiness or pain has resulted from the union of that object with the embodied Self.   And when, after many appropriations of an attractive object, it has found the result to be pain, it registers that object as one which should be avoided in the future.   "The delights that are contact-born they are verily wombs of pain." [2]

Then arises strife.   When that attractive object again presents itself, Desire throws out its harpoon and seizes it, and begins to draw it in.   The mind, remembering the painful results of previous similar captures, endeavours to check Desire, to cut with the sword of knowledge the attaching bond.   Fierce conflict rages within the man; he is dragged forward by Desire, held back by Thought; many and many a time Desire will triumph and the object will be

[1] *Light on the Path.*

[2] *Bhagavad-Gita,* v, 22.

appropriated; but the resulting pain is ever repeated, and each success of Desire arrays against it another enemy in the forces of the mind. Inevitably, however slowly, Thought proves stronger, until at last victory inclines to its side, and a day comes when the desire is weaker than the mind, and the attractive object is loosed, the attaching cord is cut. For that object, the bond is broken.

In this conflict, Thought seeks to utilize against Desire the strength of Desire. It selects objects of Desire that give a relatively lasting happiness, and seeks to utilize these against the desires that swiftly result in pain. Thus it will set artistic against sensual pleasure; it will use fame and political or social power against enjoyments of the flesh; it will stimulate the desire to please the good, to strengthen abstention from vicious delights; it will finally make the desire for eternal peace conquer the desires for temporal joys. By the one great attraction the lower attractions are slain and cease to be any longer the objects of desire: " Even taste (for them) turneth away from him after the Supreme is seen." [1] The very energy of Desire can tear it away from that which brings pain, and fix it on that which brings bliss. The same force that bound is made to serve as an instrument of freedom. Wrenching itself away from objects, it will turn upwards and

[1] *Bhagavad Gita,* ii, 59.

inwards, attaching the man to the Life whence he came forth, and in union with which consists his highest bliss.

Herein lies the value of devotion as a liberator. Love, turning to the Supreme, sees Him as eminently desirable, as an Object for intense desire, and this burns up attachments to objects that keep the heart in bondage.

Only by the Self as Thought can be mastered the Self as Desire; the Self, realizing itself as the life, overcomes the Self embodied and thinking itself to be the form. The man must learn to separate himself from the vehicles in which he desires, thinks, and acts, to know them as part of the Not-Self, as material external to life. Thus the energy that went out to objects in the lower desires becomes the higher desire guided by the mind and is prepared to be transmuted into Will.

As the lower mind merges itself in the higher, and the higher into that which is Wisdom, the aspect of pure Will emerges as the Power of the Spirit, Self-determined, Self-ruled, in perfect harmony with the Supreme Will, and therefore free. Then only are all bonds broken, and the Spirit is unconstrained by aught outside himself. Then, and then only, can the Will be said to be free.

CHAPTER III

DESIRE (*continued*)

1. THE VEHICLE OF DESIRE

WE shall have to return to the struggle in the Desire-nature, in order to add some useful details to that which has been already said; but it is first necessary to study the Vehicle of Desire, the Desire-Body or Astral Body, as this study will enable us to understand the precise method in which we may work to subdue and get rid of the lower desires.

The Vehicle of Desire is made up of what is called astral matter, the matter of the plane above the physical. This matter, like the physical, exists in seven modifications, which relatively to each other are like the solid, liquid, gaseous, etc., sub-states of matter on the physical plane. As the physical body contains within itself these various sub-states of physical matter, so does the astral body contain within itself the various sub-states of astral matter. Each of these sub-states has in it coarser and finer aggregations, and the work of astral, as of physical, purification consists in the substitution of the finer for the coarser.

Moreover, the lower sub-states of astral matter serve chiefly for the manifestation of the lower desires, while the higher sub-states vibrate in answer to the desires which have changed, by the intermixture of mind, into emotions. The lower desires, grasping after objects of pleasure, find that the lower sub-states serve as medium for their attractive force, and the coarser and baser the desires, the coarser are the aggregations of matter that fitly express them. As the desire causes the corresponding material in the astral body to vibrate, that matter becomes strongly vitalized and attracts fresh similar matter from outside to itself, and thus increases the amount of such matter in the constitution of the astral body. When the desires are gradually refined into emotions, intellectual elements entering into them, and selfishness diminishing, the amount of finer matter similarly increases in the astral body, while the coarser matter, left unvitalized, loses energy and decreases in amount.

These facts, applied to practice, help us to weaken the enemy who is enthroned within us, for we can deprive him of his instruments. A traitor within the gates is more dangerous than a foe outside, and the desire-body acts as such a traitor, so long as it

is composed of elements that answer to the temptations from without.

Desire, as it builds in the coarser materials, must
be checked by the mind, the mind refusing to
picture the passing pleasure which the possession of
the object would entail, and picturing to itself the
more lasting sorrow it would cause. As we get rid
of the coarser matter which vibrates in answer to
the baser attractions, those attractions lose all
power to disturb us.

This Vehicle of Desire, then, must be taken in
hand; according to its building will be the attractions that reach us from without. We can work
upon the form, change the elements of which the
form is composed, and thus turn the enemy into a
defender.

When a man is evolving in character, he is, however, confronted with a difficulty which often alarms
and depresses him. He finds himself shaken by
desires from which he shrinks, of which he is
ashamed, and despite his strenuous efforts to shake
them off, they none the less cling to and torment
him. They are discordant with his efforts, his
hopes, his aspirations, and yet, in some way, they
seem to be his. This painful experience is due to
the fact that the consciousness evolves more rapidly
than the form can change, and the two are to some
extent in conflict with each other. There is a

considerable amount of the coarser aggregations still present in the astral body; but as the desires have become more refined, they no longer vivify these materials. Some of the old vitality none the less persists therein, and although these aggregations are decaying they are not wholly gone.

Now although the man's Desire-nature is no longer using these materials for self-expression, they may yet be thrown into temporary activity from outside, and thus take on a semblance of vitality as a galvanized corpse might do. The desires of other people—desire-elementals of an evil kind—may attach themselves to these disused elements in his astral body, and they may thus be stimulated and revivified, and cause him to feel as his own the promptings of desires he abhors. Where such experiences are undergone, let the bewildered combatant take courage; even in the inrush of these desires, let him repudiate them as none of his, and know that the elements in him they utilize are of the past, and are dying, and that the day of their death and of his freedom is at hand.

We may take an example from dream, to show this working of effete matter in the astral body. A man, in a former life, was a drunkard, and his after-death experiences had impressed deeply on him a repulsion for drink; on rebirth, the Ego in the new physical and astral bodies impressed on them this repulsion, but there was none the less in the astral body some matter drawn thereinto by the vibrations caused in the permanent atom by the former drunkenness. This matter is not vivified in the present life by any craving for drink, nor any yeilding to the drink-habit; on the contrary, in the waking life, the man is sober. But in dream, this matter in the astral body is stimulated into activity from without, and the control of the Ego being weak over the astral body,[1] this matter responds to the drink-craving vibrations that reach it, and the man dreams that he drinks. Moreover, if there still be in the man a latent desire for drink, too weak to assert itself during waking-consciousness, it may come up in the dream-state. For physical matter being comparatively heavy and hard to move, a weak desire has not energy enough to cause vibrations therein; but that same desire may move the much lighter astral matter, and so a man may be carried away in a dream by a desire which has no power over him in his waking-consciousness. Such dreams cause much distress, because not understood. The man should understand that the dream shows that the temptation is conquered so far as he is concerned, and that he is only troubled by the corpse of past desires, vivified from outside

[1] The Ego turns his attention inward during sleep, until he is able to use his astral body independently; hence his control over it is weak.

on the astral plane, or if from within, then by a
dying desire too weak to move him in his waking
moments. The dream is a sign of a victory well-
nigh complete. At the same time it is a warning;
for it tells the man that there is still in his astral
body some matter apt to be vivified by vibrations
of the drink-craving, and that therefore he should
not place himself during waking life under conditions where such vibrations may abound. Until
such dreams have entirely ceased, the astral body
is not free from matter that is a source of danger.

2. THE CONFLICT OF DESIRE AND THOUGHT

We must now return to the struggle in the Desire-
nature, to which reference has already been made,
in order to add some necessary details.

This conflict belongs to what may be called the
middle stage of evolution, that long stage which
intervenes between the state of the man entirely
ruled by Desire, grasping all he wants, unchecked
by conscience, undisturbed by remorse, and the
state of the highly evolved spiritual man, in whom
Will, Wisdom and Activity work in co-ordinated
harmony. The conflict arises between Desire and
Thought—Thought beginning to understand the
relation of itself to the Not-Self and to other separated selves, and Desire, influenced by the objects

around it, moving by attractions and repulsions, drawn hither and thither by objects that allure.

We must study the stage of evolution in which the accumulated memories of past experiences, stored in the mind, set themselves against the gratification of desires which have been proved to lead to pain; or, to speak more accurately, in which the conclusion drawn by the Thinker from these accumulated experiences asserts itself in face of a demand from the Desire-nature for the object which has been stamped as dangerous.

The habit of grasping and enjoying has been established for hundreds of lives, and is strong, while the habit of resisting a present pleasure in order to avoid a future pain is only in course of establishment and is consequently very weak. Hence the conflicts between the Thinker and the Desire-nature end for a long time in a series of defeats. The young Mind struggling with the mature Desire body finds itself constantly vanquished. But every victory of the Desire-nature, being followed by a brief pleasure and a long pain, gives birth to a new force hostile to itself, that recruits the strength of its opponent. Each defeat of the Thinker thus sows the seeds of his future victory, and his strength daily grows while the strength of the Desire-nature diminishes.

When this is clearly understood, we grieve no longer over our own falls and falls of those we love;

for we know that these falls are making sure the secure footing of the future, and that in the womb of pain is maturing the future conqueror.

Our knowledge of right and wrong grows out of experience, and is elaborated only by trial. The sense of right and wrong, now innate in the civilized man, has been developed by innumerable experiences. In the early days of the separated Self all experiences were useful in his evolution, and brought him the lessons needful for his growth. Gradually he learned that the yielding to desires which in the course of their gratification injured others, brought him pain out of proportion to the temporary pleasure derived from their satisfaction. He began to attach the word " wrong " to the desires the yielding to which brought a predominance of pain, and this the more quickly because the Teachers who guided his early growth placed on the objects which attracted such desires the ban of Their disapproval. When he had disobeyed Them and suffering followed, the impression made on the Thinker was the more powerful for the previous fore-telling, and conscience—the Will to do the right and abstain from the wrong—was proportionately strengthened.

In this connection we can readily see the value of admonition, reproof, and good counsel. All these are stored up in the mind, and are forces added to the accumulating memories which oppose the

gratification of wrong desire. Granted that the person
warned may again yield when the temptation assails
him; that only means that the balance of strength is
still in the wrong desire; when the foretold suffering
arrives, the mind will recall all the memories of
warnings and admonitions, and will engrave the
more deeply in its substance the decision: " This
desire is wrong." The doing of the wrong act
merely means that the memory of past pain is not
yet sufficiently strong to overbear the attraction of
eagerly anticipated and immediate pleasure. The
lesson needs to be repeated yet a few times more,
to strengthen the memory of the past, and when
that is done victory is sure. The suffering is a
necessary element in the growth of the soul, and has
the promise of that growth within it. Everywhere
around us, if we see aright, is growing good; no-
where is there hopeless evil.

This struggle is expressed in the sad cry: " What
I would, that I do not; what I would not, that I
do." " When I would do good, evil is present
with me." The wrong that we do, when the wish
is against the doing, is done by the habit of the
past. The weak Will is overpowered by the strong
Desire.

Now the Thinker in his conflict with the Desire-
nature calls to his aid that very nature, and strives
to awaken in it a desire which shall be opposed to

the desire against which he is waging war. As the attraction of a weak magnet may be overpowered by that of a stronger one, so may one desire be strengthened for the overcoming of another, a right desire may be aroused to combat a wrong one. Hence the value of an ideal.

3. THE VALUE OF AN IDEAL

An ideal is a fixed mental concept of an inspiring character, framed for the guidance of conduct, and the formation of an ideal is one of the most effective means of influencing desire. The ideal may, or may not, find embodiment in an individual, according to the temperament of the man who frames it, and it must ever be remembered that the value of an ideal depends largely on its attractiveness, and that that which attracts one temperament by no means necessarily attracts another. An abstract ideal and a personal one are equally good, regarded from a general standpoint, and that should be selected which has, on the individual choosing it, the most attractive influence. A person of the intellectual temperament will usually find an abstract ideal the more satisfactory; whereas one of the emotional temperament will demand a concrete embodiment of his thought. The disadvantage of the abstract ideal is that it is apt to fail in compelling inspiration; the disadvantage of the concrete embodiment is that the embodiment is apt to fall below the ideal.

The mind, of course, creates the ideal, and either retains it as an abstraction, or embodies it in a person. The time chosen for the creation of an ideal should be a time when the mind is calm and steady and luminous, when the Desire-nature is asleep. Then the Thinker should consider the purpose of his life, the goal at which he aims, and with this to guide his choice he should select the qualities necessary to enable him to reach that goal. These qualities he should combine into a single concept, imagining as strongly as he can this integration of the qualities he needs. Daily he should repeat this integrating process, until his ideal stands out clearly in the mind, dowered with all beauty of high thought and noble character, a figure of compelling attractiveness. The man of intellect will keep this ideal as a pure concept. The man of emotional nature will embody it in a person, such as the Buddha, the Christ, Shri Krishna or some other divine Teacher. In this latter case he will, if possible, study His life, His teaching, His actions, and the ideal will thus become more and more strongly vivified, more and more real to the Thinker. Intense love will spring up in the heart for this embodied ideal, and Desire will stretch out longing arms to embrace it. And when temptation assails, and the lower desires clamour for satisfaction, then the attractive power of the ideal asserts itself, the loftier desire combats the baser, and the Thinker finds himself reinforced by right desire, the negative strength of memory which says: "Abstain from the base", being fortified by the positive strength of the ideal which says: "Achieve the heroic."

The man who lives habitually in the presence of a great ideal is armed against wrong desires by love of his ideal, by shame of being base in its presence, by the longing to resemble that which he adores, and also by the general set and trend of his mind along lines of noble thinking. Wrong desires become more and more incongruous. They perish naturally, unable to breathe in that pure clear air.

It may be worth while to remark here, in view of the destructive results of historical criticism in the minds of many, that the value of the ideal Christ, the ideal Buddha, the ideal Krishna, is in no way injured by any lack of historical data, by any defects in the proofs of the authenticity of a manuscript. Many of the stories related may not be historically true, but they are ethically and vitally true. Whether this incident happened in the physical life of this Teacher or not is a matter of small import; the reaction of such an ideal character on his environment is ever profoundly true. The world-scriptures represent spiritual facts, whether the physical incidents be or be not historically true.

Thus Thought may shape and direct Desire, and turn it from an enemy into an ally. By changing the direction of Desire, it becomes a lifting and quickening instead of a retarding force, and where desires for objects held us fast in the mire of earth, desire for the ideal lifts us on strong wings to heaven.

4. THE PURIFICATION OF DESIRE

We have already seen how much may be done in the purification of the Vehicle of Desire, and the contemplation and worship of the ideal which has just been described is a most potent means for the purification of Desire. Evil desires die away as good desires are encouraged and fostered—die away merely from want of nourishment.

The effort to reject all wrong desires is accompanied by the firm refusal of thought to allow them to pass on into actions. Will begins to restrain action, even when Desire clamours for gratification. And this refusal to permit the action instigated by wrong desire gradually deprives of all attractive power the objects which erstwhile aroused it. " The objects of sense . . . turn away from an abstemious dweller in the body." [1] The desires fade away, starved by lack of satisfaction. Abstention from gratification is a potent means of purification.

There is another means of purification in which the repulsive force of Desire is utilized, as in the contemplation of the ideal the attractive force was evoked. It is useful in extreme cases, in which the lowest desires are tumultuous and insurgent, such desires as lead to the vices of gluttony, drunkenness, and profligacy. Sometimes a man finds it impossible to get rid of evil desires, and despite all his efforts his mind yields to their strong impulse and evil imaginations riot his brain. He may conquer by apparent yielding, carrying on the evil imaginations to their inevitable results. He pictures himself yielding to the temptations that assail him, and sinking more and more into the grip of the evil that masters him. He follows himself, as he falls deeper and deeper, becoming the helpless slave of his passions. He traces with vivid imagination the stages of his descent, sees his body becoming coarser and coarser, then bloated and diseased. He contemplates the shattered nerves, the loathsome sores, the hideous decay and ruin of the once strong and healthy frame. He fixes his eyes on the dishonoured death, the sad legacy of shameful memory

[1] *Bhagavad Gita,* II, 59.

left to relatives and friends. He faces in thought the other side of death, and sees the soil and distortion of his vices pictured in the suffering astral body, and the agony of the craving of desires that may no longer be fulfilled. Resolutely he forces his shrinking thoughts to dwell on this miserable panorama of the triumph of wrong desires, until there rises within him a strong repulsion against them, an intolerable fear and loathing of the result of present yielding.

Such a method of purification is like the surgeon's knife, cutting out a cancer which menaces the life, and, like all surgical operations, is to be avoided unless no other means of cure remain. It is better to conquer wrong desire by the attractive force of an ideal than by the repulsive force of a spectacle of ruin. But where attraction fails to conquer, repulsion may perhaps prevail.

There is also a danger in this latter method, since the coarser matter in the Vehicle of Desire is increased by this dwelling in thought on evil, and the struggle is thereby rendered longer than when it is possible to throw the life into good desires and high aspirations. Therefore it is the worse method of the two, only to be accepted when the other is unattainable.

By higher attraction, by repulsion, or by the slow teaching of suffering, Desire must be purified. The " must " is not so much a necessity imposed by an outside Deity as the imperial command of the Deity within, who will not be denied. With this true Will of the Divinity, who is our Self, all divine forces in Nature work, and that divine Self who wills the highest must inevitably in the end subdue all things to himself.

With this triumph comes the ceasing of Desire. For then external objects no longer either attract or repel the outgoing energies of Atma, and these energies are entirely directed by Self-determined Wisdom; that is, Will has taken the place of Desire. Good and evil are seen as the divine forces that work for evolution, the one as necessary as the other, the one the complement of the other. The good is the force that is to be worked with; the evil is the force that is to be worked against; by the right using of both, the powers of the Self are evolved into manifestation.

When the Self has developed the aspect of Wisdom, he looks on the righteous and the wicked, the saint and the sinner, with equal eyes, and is therefore equally ready to help both, to reach out strong hands to either. Desire, which regarded them with attraction and repulsion, as pleasure-giving and pain-giving, has ceased, and Will, which is energy directed by Wisdom, brings fitting aid to both. Thus man rises above the tyranny of the pairs of opposites, and dwells in the Eternal Peace.

CHAPTER IV

EMOTION

1. THE BIRTH OF EMOTION

EMOTION is not a simple or primary state of consciousness, but is a compound made up by the interaction of two of the aspects of the Self—Desire and Intellect. The play of Intellect on Desire gives birth to Emotion; it is the child of both, and shows some of the characteristics of its father, Intellect, as well as of its mother, Desire.

In the developed condition Emotion seems so different from Desire that their fundamental identity is somewhat veiled; but we can see this identity either by tracing the development of a desire into an emotion, or by studying both side by side, and finding that both have the same characteristics, the same divisions, that the one is in fact an elaborated form of the other, the elaboration due to the presence in the later of a number of intellectual elements absent from, or less markedly prominent in, the earlier.

Let us trace the development of a desire into an emotion in one of the commonest of human relations, the relation of sex. Here is desire in one of its simplest forms; desire for food, desire for sexual union, are the two fundamental desires of all living things—desire for food to maintain life, desire for sexual union to increase life. In both the sense of " moreness " is experienced, or, otherwise stated, pleasure is felt. The desire for food remains a desire; the food is appropriated, assimilated, loses its separate identity, becomes part of the " Me ". There is no continued relation between the eater and the food which gives scope for the elaboration of an emotion. It is otherwise in the sex-relation, which tends to become more and more permanent with the evolution of the individuality.

Two savages are drawn towards each other by the attraction of sex; a passion to possess the other arises in each; each desires the other. The desire is as simple as the desire for food. But it cannot be satisfied to the same extent, for neither can wholly appropriate and assimilate the other; each to some extent maintains his or her separate identity, and each only partially becomes the " Me " of the other. There is indeed an extension of the " Me ", but it is by way of inclusion and not by way of self-identification. The presence of this persisting barrier is necessary for the transformation of a desire into an emotion. This makes possible the attachment of memory and anticipation to the same object, and not to another object similar in kind—as in the case of food. A continuing desire for union with the same object becomes an emotion, thoughts thus mingling with the primary desire to possess. The barrier which keeps the mutually attracted objects as two, not one, which prevents their fusion, while it seems to frustrate really immortalizes; were it swept away, desire and emotion alike would vanish, and the Twain-become-One must then seek another external object for the further self-expansion of pleasure.

To return to our savages, desire-united. The woman falls sick, and ceases, for the time, to be an object of sex-gratification. But the man remembers past, and anticipates future, delight, and a feeling of sympathy with her suffering, of compassion for her weakness, arises within him. The persisting attraction towards her, due to memory and antici-pation, changes desire into emotion, passion into love, and sympathy and compassion are its earliest manifestations. These, in turn, will lead to his sacrificing himself to her, waking to nurse her when he would sleep, exerting himself for her when he would rest. These spontaneous moods of the love-emotion in him will later solidify into virtues, i.e., will become permanent moods in his character, showing themselves in response to the calls of human need to all persons with whom he comes into contact, whether they attract him or not. We shall see later that virtues are simply permanent moods of right emotion.

Before, however, dealing with the relation of ethics and emotion, we must further realize the fundamental identity of Desire and Emotion by noting their characteristics and divisions. As this is done, we shall find that emotions do not form a mere jungle, but that all spring from one root, dividing into two main stems, each of these again sub-dividing into branches, on which grow the leaves of virtues and of vices. This fruitful idea, making possible a science of the emotions, and hence an intelligible and rational system of ethics, is due to an Indian author, Bhagavan Das, who has for the first time introduced order into this hitherto confused region of consciousness. Students of psychology will find in his *Science of the Emotions* a lucid treatise, setting forth this scheme, which reduces the chaos of the emotions into a cosmos, and shapes therein an ordered morality. The broad lines of exposition followed here are drawn from that work, to which readers are referred for fuller details.

We have seen that Desire has two main expressions: desire to attract, in order to possess, or again to come into contact with, any object which has previously afforded pleasure; desire to repel, in order to drive far away, or to avoid contact with, any object which has previously inflicted pain. We have seen that Attraction and Repulsion are the two forms of Desire, swaying the Self.

Emotion, being Desire infused with Intellect, inevitably shows the same division into two. The Emotion which is of the nature of Attraction, attracting objects to each other by pleasure, the integrating energy in the universe, is called Love. The Emotion which is of the nature of Repulsion, driving objects apart from each other by pain, the disintegrating energy in the universe, is called Hate. These are the two stems from the root of Desire, and all the branches of the emotions may be traced back to one of these twain.

Hence the identity of the characteristics of Desire and Emotion; Love seeks to draw to itself the attractive object, or to go after it, in order to unite with it, to possess, or be possessed by, it. It binds by pleasure, by happiness, as Desire binds. Its ties are indeed more lasting, more complicated, are composed of more numerous and more delicate threads interwoven into greater complexity, but the essence of Desire-Attraction, the binding of two objects together, is the essence of Emotion-Attraction, of Love. And so also does Hate seek to drive away from itself the repellent object, or to flee from it, in order to be apart from it, to repulse, or be

18

repulsed by, it. It separates by pain, by unhappiness. And thus the essence of Desire-Repulsion, the driving apart of two objects, is the essence of Emotion-Repulsion, of Hate. Love and Hate are the elaborated and thought-infused forms of the simple Desires to possess and to shun.

2. The Play of Emotion in the Family

Man has been described as " a social animal "—the biological way of saying that he develops best in contact with, not in isolation from, his fellows. His distinctively intellectual characteristics need, for their evolution, a social medium, and his keenest pleasures—and hence necessarily his keenest pains —arise in his relations with others of his own species. They alone can evoke from him the responses on which his further growth depends. All evolution, all the calling out of latent powers, is in response to stimuli from without, and, when the human stage is reached, the most poignant and effective stimuli can only come from contacts with human beings.

Sex-attraction is the first social bond, and the children born to the husband and wife form with them the first social unit, the family. The prolonged helplessness and dependence of the human infant give time for the physical passion of parentage to ripen into the emotion of maternal and paternal love, and thus give stability to the family, while the family itself forms a field in which the various emotions inevitably play. Herein are first established definite and permanent relations between human beings, and on the harmony of these relations, on the benefits bestowed by these relations on each member of the family, does the happiness of each depend.

We can advantageously study the play of Emotion in the family, since here we have a comparatively simple social unit, which yet affords a picture in miniature of society at large. We can find here the origin and evolution of virtues and vices, and see the meaning and object of morality.

We have already seen how sex-passion evolves under stress of circumstances into the emotion of love, and how this love shows itself as tenderness and compassion when the wife, instead of being the equal mate, becomes helpless and dependent, in the temporary physical inferiority caused, say, by child bearing. Similarly should sickness or accident reduce the husband to temporary physical inferiority, tenderness and compassion will flow out to him from the wife. But these manifestations of love cannot be shown by the stronger without evoking from the weaker answering love-manifestations; these in the condition of weakness will have as their natural characteristics trust, confidence, gratitude, all equally love-emotions coloured by weakness and dependence. In the relation of parents to children and of children to parents, where physical superiority and inferiority are far more strongly marked and persist for a considerable period of time, these love-emotions will be continually manifested on both sides. Tenderness, compassion, protection, will be constantly shown by the parents to the children, and trust, confidence, gratitude, will be the constant answer of the children. Variations in the expression of the love-emotion will be caused by variety of circumstances, which will call out generosity, forgiveness, patience, etc., on the part of the parents, and obedience, dutifulness, serviceableness, etc., on the part of the children. Taking these two classes of love-emotions, we see that the common essence in the one class is benevolence, and in the other reverence; the first is love looking downwards on those weaker, inferior to itself; the other, love looking upwards on those stronger, superior to itself. And we can then generalize and say: Love looking downwards is Benevolence; Love looking upwards is Reverence; and these are the several common characteristics of Love from superiors to inferiors, and Love from inferiors to superiors universally.

The normal relations between husband and wife, and those between brothers and sisters, afford us the field for studying the manifestations of love between equals. We see love showing itself as mutual tenderness and mutual trustfulness, as consideration, respect, and desire to please, as quick insight into and endeavour to fulfil the wishes of the other, as magnanimity, forbearance. The elements present in the love-emotions of superior to inferior are found here, but mutuality is impressed on all of them. So we may say that the common characteristic of love between equals is Desire for Mutual Help.

Thus we have Benevolence, Desire for Mutual Help, and Reverence as the three main divisions of the Love-Emotion, and under these all love-emotions may be classified. For all human relations are summed up under the three classes: the relations of superiors to inferiors, of equals to equals, of inferiors to superiors.

A similar study of the Hate-Emotion in the family will yield us similar fruits. Where there is hate between husband and wife, the temporary superior will show harshness, cruelty, oppression to the temporary inferior, and these will be answered by the inferior with hate-manifestations characteristic of weakness, such as vindictiveness, fear, and treachery. These will be even more apparent in the relations between parents and children, when both are dominated by the Hate-Emotion, since the disparity is here greater, and tyranny breeds a whole crop of evil emotions—deceit, servility, cowardice, while the child is helpless, and disobedience, revolt, and revenge as it grows older. Here again we seek a common characteristic, and find that Hate looking downwards is Scorn, and looking upwards is Fear.

Similarly, Hate between equals will show itself in anger, combativeness, disrespect, violence, aggressiveness, jealousy, insolence, etc.—all the emotions which repel man from man when they stand as rivals, face to face, not hand in hand. The common characteristic of Hate between equals will thus be Mutual Injury. And the three main characteristics of the Hate-Emotion are Scorn, Desire for Mutual Injury, and Fear.

Love is characterized in all its manifestations by sympathy, self-sacrifice, the desire to give; these are its essential factors, whether as Benevolence, as Desire for Mutual Help, as Reverence. For all these directly serve Attraction, bring about union, are of the very nature of Love. Hence Love is of the Spirit; for sympathy is the feeling for another as one would feel for oneself; self-sacrifice is the recognition of the claim of the other, as oneself; giving is the condition of spiritual life. Thus Love is seen to belong to the Spirit, to the life-side of the universe.

Hate, on the other hand, is characterized in all its manifestations by antipathy, self-aggrandisement, the desire to take; these are its essential factors, whether as Scorn, Desire for Mutual Injury, or Fear. All these directly serve Repulsion, driving one apart from another. Hence, Hate is of Matter, emphasises manifoldness and differences, is essentially separateness, belongs to the form-side of the universe.

We have thus far dealt with the play of Emotion in the family, because the family serves as a miniature of society. Society is only the integration of numerous family units, but the absence of the blood-tie between these units, the absence of recognized common interests and common objects, makes it necessary to find some bond which will supply the place of the natural bonds in the family. The family units in a society appear on the surface as rivals, rather than as brothers and sisters; hence the Hate-Emotion is more likely to rise than the Love-Emotion, and it is necessary to find some way of maintaining harmony; this is done by the transmutation of love-emotions into virtues.

3. THE BIRTH OF VIRTUES

We have seen that when members of a family pass beyond the small circle of relatives, and meet people whose interests are either indifferent or opposed to them, there is not between them and the others the mutual interplay of Love. Rather does Hate show itself, ranging from the watchful attitude of suspicion to the destroying fury of war. How then is a society to be composed of the separate family units?

It can only be done by making permanent all the emotional moods which spring from Love, and by eradicating those which spring from Hate. A permanent mood of a love-emotion directed towards a living being is a Virtue; a permanent mood of a hate-emotion directed against a living being is a Vice. This change is wrought by the Intellect, which bestows on the emotion a permanent character, seeking harmony in all relations in order that happiness may result. That which conduces to harmony and therefore to happiness in the family, springing spontaneously from Love, is Virtue when practised towards all in every relation of life. Virtue springs from Love, and its result is happiness. So also that which conduces to disharmony and therefore to misery in the family, springing spontaneously from Hate, is Vice when practised towards all in all relations of life.

An objection is raised to this theory, that the permanent mood of a love-emotion is a virtue, by pointing out that adultery, theft, and other vices may spring from the love-emotion. Here analysis of the elements entering into the mental attitude is necessary. It is complex, not simple. The act of adultery is motived by love, but not by love alone. There enter into it also contempt of the honour of another, indifference to the happiness of another, the selfish grasping at personal pleasure at the cost of social stability, social honour, social decency. All these spring from hate-emotions. The love is the one redeeming feature in the whole transaction, the one virtue in the bundle of sordid vices. Similar analysis will always show that when the exercise of a love-emotion is wrong, the wrongness lies in the vice bound up with its exercise, and not in the love-emotion itself.

4. Right and Wrong

Let us now turn, for a moment, to the question of Right and Wrong, and see the relation they bear to bliss and misery. For there is an idea widely current that there is something low and materialistic in the view that virtue is the means to bliss. Many think that this idea degrades virtue, giving it the second place where it should hold the first, and making it a means instead of an end. Let us then see why virtue must be the path to bliss, and how this inheres in the nature of things.

When the Intellect studies the world, and sees the innumerable relations established therein, and

observes that harmonious relations bring about
happiness and that jarring relations bring about
misery, it sets to work to find out the way of estab-
lishing universal harmony and hence universal bliss.
Further, it discovers that the world is moving along
a path which it is compelled to tread—the path of
evolution, and it finds out the law of evolution.
For a part, a unit, to set itself with the law of the
whole to which it belongs means peace, harmony,
and therefore happiness, while for it to set itself
against that law means friction, disharmony, and
therefore misery. Hence the Right is that which,
being in harmony with the great law, brings bliss,
and the Wrong is that which, being in conflict with
the great law, brings misery. When the Intellect,
illuminated by the Spirit, sees Nature as an expression of divine Thought, the law of evolution as an
expression of the divine Will, the goal as an expression of divine Bliss, then for harmony with the law
of evolution we may substitute harmony with the
divine Will, and the Right becomes that which is in
harmony with the Will of God, and morality becomes
permeated with religion.

5. VIRTUE AND BLISS

Perfection, harmony with the divine Will, cannot
be separated from bliss. Virtue is the road to bliss,

and if anything does not lead there it is not virtue. The perfection of the divine nature expresses itself in harmony, and when the scattered " divine fragments " come into harmony they taste bliss.

This fact is sometimes veiled by another, i.e., that the practice of a virtue under certain circumstances brings about misery. That is true, but the misery is temporary and superficial, and the balance between that outer misery and the inner bliss arising from the virtuous conduct, is in favour of the latter; and further, the misery is not due to the virtue but to the circumstances which oppose its practice, to the friction between the good organism and the evil environment. So when you strike a harmonious chord amid a mass of discords, for a moment it increases the discord. The virtuous man is thrown into conflict with evil, but this should not blind us to the fact that bliss is ever wedded indissolubly to Right and misery to Wrong. Even though the righteous may suffer temporarily, nothing but righteousness can lead to bliss. And if we examine the consciousness of the righteous, we find that he is happier in doing the right though superficial pain may result, than in doing the wrong which would ruffle the inner peace. The commission of a wrong act would cause him inner anguish outweighing the external pleasure. Even in the case where righteousness leads to external suffering, the suffering is less than would be caused by unrighteousness. Miss Helen Taylor has well said that for the man who dies for the sake of truth, death is easier than life with falsehood. It is easier and pleasanter for the righteous man to die as a martyr than to live as a hypocrite.

Since the nature of the Self is bliss, and that bliss is only hindered in manifestation by resisting circumstances, that which removes the friction between itself and these circumstances and opens its onward way must lead to its Self-realization, *i.e.*, to the realization of bliss. Virtue does this, and therefore virtue is a means to bliss. Where the inner nature of things is peace and joy, the harmony which permits that nature to unveil itself must bring peace and joy, and to bring about this harmony is the work of virtue.

6. THE TRANSMUTATION OF EMOTIONS INTO VIRTUES AND VICES

We have now to see more fully the truth of what was said above, that virtue grows out of emotion, and how far it is true that a virtue or a vice is merely a permanent mood of an emotion. Our definition is that virtue is a permanent mood of the love-emotion, and vice a permanent mood of the hate-emotion.

The emotions belonging to love are the constructive energies which, drawing people together, build up the family, the tribe, the nation. Love is a manifestation of attraction, and hence holds objects together. This process of integration begins with the family, and the relations, established between its members in the common life of the family entail, if there is to be happiness, the acting towards each other in a helpful and kindly way. The obligations necessary for the establishment of happiness in these relations are called duties, that which is due from one to the other. If these duties are not discharged the family relations become a source of misery, since the close contacts of the family make the happiness of each dependent on the treatment of him by the others. No relation can be entered into between human beings which does not establish an obligation between them, a duty of each towards the other. The husband loves the wife, the wife the husband, and nothing more is needed to lead each to seek the other's happiness than the intense spontaneous wish to make the beloved happy. This leads the one who can give to supply what the other needs. In the fullest sense, " love is the fulfilling of the law "; [1] there is no need for the feeling of an obligation, for love seeks ever to help and to bless, and there is no need for " thou shalt", or " thou shalt not".

[1] *Rom.*, xiii, 10.

But when a person, moved by love to discharge all the duties of his relation with another, comes into relation with those he does not love, how is a harmonious relation with them to be established? By recognizing the obligations of the relation into which he has entered, and discharging them. The doings which grew out of love in the one case present themselves as obligations; as duties, in the other, where love is not present. Right reason works the spontaneous actions of love into permanent obligations, or duties, and the love-emotion, made a permanent element of conduct, is called a virtue. This is the justification of the statement that a virtue is the permanent mood of a love-emotion. A permanent state of emotion is established which will show itself when a relation is made; the man discharges the duties of that relation; he is a virtuous man. He is moved by emotions made permanent by the intellect, which recognizes that happiness depends on the establishment of harmony in all relations. Love, rationalized and fixed by the intellect, is virtue.

In this way may be built up a science of ethics, of which the laws are as much an inevitable sequence as those on which any other science is built.

So also between the hate-emotion and vices there is a similar relation. The permanent mood of a hate-emotion is a vice. One person injures another, and the second returns the injury; the relation between these two is inharmonious, productive of misery. And as each expects injury from the other, each tries to weaken the other's power to inflict injury, and this is the spontaneous action of hate. When this mood becomes permanent, and a man shows it in any relation into which he enters wherein the opportunity for its manifestation arises, then it is called a vice. A man of uncontrolled passions and undeveloped nature strikes a blow, a spontaneous expression of hate. He repeats this often, and it becomes habitual when he is angry. He inflicts pain and takes pleasure in the infliction. The vice of cruelty is developed, and if he meets a child or a person weaker than himself, he will show cruelty merely because he comes into relation with them. As the love-emotion, guided and fixed by right reason, is virtue, so the hate-emotion, guided and fixed by distorted and blinded reason, is vice.

7. APPLICATION OF THE THEORY OF CONDUCT

When the nature of virtue and vice is thus seen, it is clear that the shortest way of strengthening the virtues and eliminating the vices is to work directly on the emotional side of the character. We can strive to develop the love-emotion, thus affording the material which the reason will elaborate into its characteristic virtues. The development of the love-emotion is the most effective way of evolving the moral character, virtues being but the blossoms and the fruits which spring from the root of love.

The value of this clear view of the transmutation of emotion into virtues and vices lies in the fact that it gives us a definite theory on which we can work; it is as though we were seeking a distant place, and a map were placed before our eyes; we trace thereon the road which leads from our present position to our goal. So many really good and earnest people spend years in vague aspirations after goodness, and yet make but little progress; they are good in purpose but weak in attainment; this is chiefly because they do not understand the nature in which they are working, and the best methods for its culture. They are like a child in a garden, a child eager to see his garden brilliant with flowers, but without the knowledge to plant and cultivate them, and to exterminate the weeds which overgrow his plot. Like the child, they long for the sweetness of the virtue-flowers, and find their garden overrun with the rank growth of the weeds of vice.

8. THE USES OF EMOTION

The uses of the love-emotion are so obvious that it seems scarcely necessary to dwell upon them, and yet too much stress cannot be laid on the fact that love is the constructive force in the universe. Having drawn together the family units, it welds these into larger tribal and national units, and these it will build in the future into the Brotherhood of Man. Nor must we omit to note the fact that the smaller units draw out the love-power and prepare it for fuller expression. Their use is to call into manifestation the hidden divine power of love within the Spirit, by giving to it objects close at hand that attract it. The love is not to be confined within these narrow limits, but as it gains strength by practice it is to spread outwards until it embraces all sentient beings. We may formulate the law of love: Regard every aged person as your father or mother; regard every person of similar age as your brother or sister; regard every younger person as your child. This sums up human relations. The fulfilment of this law would render earth a paradise, and it is in order that the earth may become such a paradise that the family exists.

A man who would widen his love-relations should begin to regard the welfare of his community as he regards the welfare of his own family. He should try to work for the public good of his community with the energy and interest with which he works for his family. Later, he will extend his loving interest and labour to his nation. Then appears the great virtue of public spirit, the sure precursor of national prosperity. Later still, he will love and labour for humanity, and finally he will embrace within his loving care all sentient beings and will become " the friend of every creature ".

Few, at the present stage of evolution, are really able to love humanity, and too many speak of loving humanity who are not ready to make any sacrifice to help a suffering brother or sister close at hand. The servant of humanity, must not overlook the human beings at his door, nor in imagination water with sentimental sympathy the distant garden, while the plants round his doorway are dying from drought.

The uses of hate are not at first so obvious, but are none the less important. At first, when we study hate and see that its essence is disintegration, destruction, it may seem all evil; " He who hateth his brother is a murderer," saith a great Teacher,[1] because murder is but an expression of hate; and even when hate does not go so far as murder it is still a destroying force; it breaks up the family, the nation, and wherever it goes it tears people apart. Of what use, then, is hate?

First, it drives apart incongruous elements, unfit to combine together, and thus prevents continuing friction. Where incongruous undeveloped people are concerned, it is better for them to be driven far

[1] *S. John*, ii. 15.

apart to pursue their several paths in evolution than to be kept within reach of one another, stimulating each other to increased bad emotions. Secondly, the repulsion felt by the average soul for an evil person is beneficial, so long as that evil person has the power of leading him astray; for that repulsion, although it be hate, guards him from an influence under which he might otherwise succumb. Contempt for the liar, the hypocrite, the worker of cruelty on the weak, is an emotion useful to the one who feels it, and also to the one against whom it is directed; for it tends to preserve the one from falling into similar vices, and it tends to arouse in the despised person a feeling of shame that may lift him from the mire in which he is plunged. So long as a person has any tendency to a sin, so long is hatred against those who practise the sin protective and useful. Presently, as he evolves, he will distinguish between the evil-doer and the evil, and will pity the evil-doer and confine his hatred to the evil. Later still, secure in virtue, he will hate neither the evil-doer nor his evil, but will see tranquilly a low stage of evolution, out of which he will strive to lift his younger brother by fitting means. " Righteous indignation", " noble scorn", " just wrath", all are phrases which recognize the usefulness of these emotions, while seeking to veil the fact that they are essentially forms of hate—a veiling which is due to the feeling that hate is an evil thing. None the less are they essentially forms of hate, whatever they may be called, though they play a useful part in evolution and purify the social atmosphere. Intolerance of evil is far better than indifference to it, and until a man is beyond the reach of temptation to any given sin, intolerance of those who practise it is for him a necessary safeguard.

Let us take the case of a man little evolved; he desires to avoid gross sins, but yet feels tempted to them. The desire to avoid them will show itself as hatred of those in whom he sees them; to check this hatred would be to plunge him into temptations he is not yet strong enough to resist. As he evolves further and further from the danger of yielding to temptation, he will hate the sins, but will pityingly sympathize with the sinner. Not till he has become a saint can he afford not to hate the evil.

When in ourselves we feel repulsion from a person we may be sure that we have in us some lingering traces of that which we dislike in him. The Ego, seeing a danger, drags his vehicles away. A man, perfectly temperate, feels less repulsion towards the drunkard than a temperate man who occasionally exceeds. A woman, utterly pure, feels no repulsion from a fallen sister, from whose contact the less pure would withdraw their skirts. When we reach perfection, we shall love the sinner as well as the saint, and perchance may show the love more to the sinner, since the saint can stand alone but the sinner will fall if he be not loved.

When the man has risen to the point where he hates neither sinner nor sin, then the disintegrating force—which is hate among human beings—becomes simply an energy to be used for destroying the obstacles which embarrass the path of evolution. When perfected wisdom guides the constructive and destructive energies, and perfected love is the motive power, then only can the destructive force be used without incurring the root-sin of the feeling of separateness. To feel ourselves different from others is the "great heresy", for separateness, when the whole is evolving towards unity, is opposition to the Law. The feeling of separateness is definitely wrong, whether it leads to one's thinking oneself more righteous or more sinful. The perfect saint identifies with the criminal as much as with another saint, for the criminal and the saint are alike divine, although in different stages of evolution. When a man can feel thus, he touches the life of the Christ in man. He does not think of himself as separate, but as one with all. To him his own holiness is the holiness of humanity, and the sin of any is his sin. He builds no barrier between himself and the sinner, but pulls down any barrier made by the sinner, and shares the sinner's evil while sharing with him his good.

Those who can feel the truth of this " counsel of perfection " should, in their daily lives, seek to practise it, however imperfectly. In dealing with the less advanced, they should ever seek to level the dividing wall. For the sense of separateness is subtle and endures till we achieve Christhood. Yet by this effort we may gradually lessen it, and to strive to identify ourselves with the lowest is to exercise the constructive energy which holds the worlds together, and to become channels for the divine love.

CHAPTER V

EMOTION (*Continued*)

1. THE TRAINING OF EMOTION

EMOTION is, we have seen, the motive power in man; it stimulates thought; it impels to action; it is as steam to the engine; without it man would be inert, passive. But there are many who are the continual prey of their emotions; who are hurried hither and thither by emotions, as a rudderless ship by stormy winds upon the ocean; who are tossed high and dragged low by surges of joyous and painful feelings; who alternate between exaltation and despair. Such a person is swayed, subjugated by emotions, continually harassed by their conflict. He is more or less a chaos within, and is erratic in his outward actions, moved by the impulse of the moment, without due consideration for surrounding circumstances, such consideration as would make his actions well directed. He is often what is called a good person, inspired by generous motives, stirred into kindly actions, full of sympathy with suffering and eager to bring relief, plunging quickly into action intended to aid the sufferer. We have not here to do with the indifferent or the cruel, but with one whose emotions hurry him into action, before he has considered the conditions or forecast the results of his activity beyond the immediate relief of the pain before his view. Such a person— though moved by a desire to help, though the stimulating emotion is sympathy and desire to relieve suffering—often does more harm than good in consequence of the inconsiderateness of his action. The emotion which impels him springs from the love-side of his nature, from the side which draws people together, and which is the root of the constructive and preserving virtues; and in this very fact lies the danger of such a person. If the emotion had its root in evil he would be the first to eradicate it; but just because it is rooted in that love-emotion whence spring all the social virtues, he does not suspect it, he does not endeavour to control. "I am so sympathetic; I am so much moved by suffering; I cannot bear the sight of misery." In all such phrases, a certain self-praise is implied, though the tone may be one of deprecation. Truly, sympathy is admirable, *qua* sympathy, but its ill-directed exercise is often provocative of mischief. Sometimes it injures the very object of sympathy, and leaves him finally in worse case than at first. Too often unwise forms of relief are adopted, more to remove the pain of the sympathizer than to cure the ill of the sufferer, and a momentary pang is stopped at the cost of a lasting injury, really, though not avowedly, to relieve the pain of the onlooker. The reaction of sympathy on the sympathetic person is good, deepening the love-emotion; but the action on others is too often bad owing to the lack of balanced thought. It is easy at the sight of pain to fill earth and sky with our shrieks, till all the air is throbbing; it is hard to pause, to measure the cause of pain and the cure, and then to apply a remedy which heals instead of perpetuating. Right Reason must govern and direct emotion if good is to result from its exercise. Emotion should be the impulse to action, but not its director; direction belongs to the intelligence, and its guiding prerogative should never be wrenched away from it. Where the consciousness thus works, having strong emotion as the impulse and right reason as director, there is the sympathetic and wise man who is useful to his generation.

Desires have been well compared to horses harnessed to the chariot of the body, and desires are rooted in emotions. Where the emotions are uncontrolled they are like plunging, unbroken horses that imperil the safety of the chariot and threaten the life of the charioteer. The reins have been compared to the mind, the reins that guide the horses, restraining or loosening as is needed. There is well imaged the relationship between emotion, intelligence, and action. Emotion gives the movement, intelligence controls and guides, and then the Self will use activity to the best advantage, as becomes the ruler of the emotions, not their victim.

With the development of that aspect of consciousness which will show itself as Buddhi in the sixth sub-race, and more completely in the sixth Root Race, the emotional nature rapidly evolves in some of the advanced fifth Race, and often for a time offers many troublesome and even distressing symptoms. As evolution proceeds, these will be outgrown, and the nature will become balanced as well as strong, wise as well as generous; meanwhile the rapidly developing nature will be stormy and often distressful, and will suffer keenly and long. Yet in those very sufferings lies its future strength as its present purification, and in proportion to the sharpness of the sufferings will be the greatness of the result. It is in these powerful natures that Buddhi is struggling to birth, and the anguish of the travail is upon them. Presently Buddhi, the Christ, the "little child", will be born, Wisdom and Love in one, and this, united to high intelligence, is the spiritual Ego, the true Inner Man, the Ruler Immortal.

The student, who is studying his own nature in order to take his own evolution in hand and direct its future course, must carefully observe his own strength and his own weakness, in order to regulate the one and correct the other. In unevenly developed persons intellect and emotion are apt to vary in inverse ratio to each other; strong emotions go with weak intelligence, and strong intelligence with weak emotions; in one case, the directing power is weak, in other the motive. The student then in his self-analysis must see whether his intelligence is well-developed, if he finds his emotions to be strong; he must test himself to discover whether he is unwilling to look at things in " the clear dry light of intellect "; if he feels repelled when a subject is presented to him in this light, he may rest assured that the emotional side of his nature is over-developed in proportion to the intellectual side. For the well-balanced man would resent neither the clear light of the directing intelligence, nor the strong force of the motive emotion. If in the past one side has been over-cultivated, if the emotions have been fostered to the detriment of the intelligence, then the efforts should be turned to the strengthening of the intellect, and the resentment which arises against a coldly intellectual presentation should be sternly curbed, the difference between intelligence and sympathy being recognized.

2. THE DISTORTING FORCE OF EMOTION

One of the things most apt to be overlooked by the emotional person is the way in which emotion fills his surrounding atmosphere with its vibrations, and thereby biasses the intelligence; everything is seen through this atmosphere and is coloured and distorted by it, so that things do not reach the intelligence in their true form and colour, but arrive twisted and discoloured. Our aura surrounds us, and should be a pellucid medium through which all in the outer world should reach us in its own form and colour; but when the aura is vibrating with emotion it cannot act as such a medium, and all is refracted that passes into it, and reaches us quite other than it is. If a person is under water and a stick is put near him in the air, and he tries to touch it his hand will be wrongly directed, for he will put his hand to the place at which he sees the stick, and as the rays coming from it are refracted on entering the water, the stick will be, for him, displaced. Similarly when an impression from the outer world reaches us, through an aura overcharged with emotion, its proportions are distorted and its position misjudged; hence the data supplied to the intelligence are erroneous, and the judgment founded upon them will therefore necessarily be wrong, however accurately the intelligence may work.

Even the most careful self-analysis will not entirely protect us against this emotional disturbance. The intellect ever tends to judge favourably that which we like, unfavourably that which we dislike, owing to the " refraction " above-named. The arguments in favour of a certain course are thrown into a strong light by our desire to follow it, and the arguments against it are thrown into the shade. The one seems so clear and forcible, the other so dubious and feeble. And to our mind, seeing through the emotion, it is so sure that we are right, and that anyone who does not see as we do is biassed by prejudice or is wilfully perverse. Against this ever-present danger we can only guard by care and persistent effort, but we cannot finally escape it until we transcend the emotions and become absolutely their ruler.

One way remains in which we can aid ourselves to a right judgment, and that is by studying the workings of consciousness in others, and in weighing their decisions under circumstances similar to our own. The judgments which most repel us are those most likely to be useful to us, because made through an emotional medium very different from our own. We can compare their decisions with ours, and by noting the points that affect them most and ourselves least, and that weigh most heavily with us and most lightly with them, we may disentangle the emotional from the intellectual elements in the judgments. And even where our conclusions are mistaken the effort to arrive at them is corrective and illuminative; it aids in the mastery of the emotions and strengthens the intellectual element. Such studies should of course be made when there is no emotional disturbance, and its fruits should be stored up for use at the times when the emotions are strong.

3. METHODS OF RULING THE EMOTIONS

The first and most powerful method for obtaining mastery of the emotions is—as in all that touches consciousness—Meditation. Before contact with the world has disturbed the emotions, meditation should be resorted to. Coming back into the body after the period of physical sleep, from a world subtler than the physical, the Ego will find his tenement quiet and can take possession calmly of the rested brain and nerves. Meditation later in the day, when the emotions have been disturbed and when they are in full activity, is not as efficacious. The quiet time which is available after sleep is the right season for effective meditation, the desire-body, the emotional nature, being more tranquil than after it has plunged into the bustle of the world. From that peaceful morning hour will stream out the influence which will guard during the day, and the emotions, soothed and stilled, will be more amenable to control.

Where it is possible, it is well to forecast the questions which may arise during the day, and to come to conclusions as to the view to be taken, the conduct to be pursued. If we know that we shall be placed under certain conditions that will arouse our emotions, we can decide beforehand on our mental attitude and even come to a decision on our action. Supposing such a decision has been reached, then when the circumstances arise that decision should be recalled and acted upon, even though the swell of the emotions may impel towards a different course. For instance, we are going to meet a person for whom we have a strong affection, and we decide in our meditation on the course that it is wisest to pursue, deciding in the clear light of calm intelligence what is best for all concerned. To this decision we should adhere, even though there is the inclination to feel: " I had not given the proper weight to that view." As a matter of fact under these conditions overweight is given, the proper weight having been given in the calmer thought; and it is the wisest plan to follow the path previously chalked out, despite the emotional promptings of the moment. There may be a blunder of judgment, but if the blunder be not seen during meditation it is not likely to be seen during a swirl of emotions.

Another method of curbing the emotions is to think over what is going to be said before speaking, to put a bridle on the tongue. The man who has learned to control his speech has conquered everything, says an ancient eastern lawgiver. The person who never speaks a sharp or ill-considered word is well on the way to control emotion. To rule speech is to rule the whole nature. It is a good plan not to speak—to deliberately check speech—until one is clear as to what one is going to say, is sure that the speech is true, that it is adapted to the person to whom it is to be addressed, and that it is such as ought to be spoken. Truth comes first and foremost, and nothing can excuse falsity of speech; many a speech uttered under stress of emotion is false, either from exaggeration or distortion. Then, the appropriateness of the speech to the person addressed is too often forgotten, in the hurry of emotion or the eagerness of strong feeling. A quite wrong idea of a great truth may be presented if the point of view of the person addressed is not borne in mind; sympathy is needed, the seeing as he sees, for only then can the truth be useful and helpful. One is not trying to help oneself, but to help another, in putting the truth before him. Perhaps the conception of law as changeless, inviolable, absolutely impartial, may to the speaker be inspiring, strengthening, uplifting; whereas that conception is ruthless and crushing to an undeveloped person, and injures instead of helps. Truth is not meant to crush but to elevate, and we misuse truth when we give it to one that is not ready. There is plenty to suit the needs of each, but discretion is needed to choose wisely, and enthusiasm must not force a premature enlightenment. Many a young Theosophist does more harm than good by his over-eager pressing on others of the treasures he prizes so highly. Lastly, the form of the speech, the necessity or the usefulness of its utterance, should be considered. A truth that might help may be changed into a truth that hinders by the way in which it is put. "Never speak what is untrue, never speak what is unpleasant," is a golden rule of speech. All speech should be truthful, sweet, and agreeable. This agreeableness of speech is too often forgotten by well-meaning people, who even pride themselves on their candour when they are merely rude and indifferent to the feelings of those whom they address. But that is neither good breeding nor religion, for the unmannerly is not the religious. Religion combines perfect truth with perfect courtesy. Moreover, the superfluous, the useless, is mischievous, and there is much injury done by the continual bubbling over of frivolous

20

emotions in chatter and small talk. People who cannot bear silence and are ever chattering fritter away their intellectual and moral forces, as well as give utterance to a hundred follies better left unsaid. To be afraid of silence is a sign of mental weakness, and calm silence is better than foolish speech. In silence the emotions grow and strengthen while remaining controlled, and thus the motive power of the nature increases and is also brought into subjection. The power of being silent is great and often exercises a most soothing effect; on the other hand, he who has learned to be silent must be careful that his silence does not trench on his courtesy, that he does not, by inappropriate silence among others, make them feel chilled and uncomfortable.

Some may fear that such a consideration before speech as is outlined may so hinder exchange of thought as to paralyze conversation; but all who have practised such control will bear witness that after a brief practice no noticeable interval is caused before the reply is uttered. Swifter than lightning is the movement of the intelligence, and it will flash over the points to be considered while a breath is being drawn. It is true that at first there will be slight hesitation, but in a few weeks no pause will be required, and the review of the proposed utterance will be made too swiftly to cause any obstruction.

Many an orator can testify that in the rapid torrent of a declamatory period the mind will sit at ease, turning about alternative sentences and weighing their respective merits ere one is chosen and the rest are cast aside; and yet none in the rapt audience will know aught of this by-play, or dream that behind the swift utterance there is any such selective action going on.

A third method of mastering emotion is by refraining from acting on impulse. The hurry to act is characteristic of the modern mind, and is the excess of the promptitude which is its virtue. When we consider life calmly we realize that there is never any need for hurry; there is always time enough, and action, however swift, should be well considered and unhurried. When an impulse comes from some strong emotion and we spring forward in obedience without consideration, we act unwisely. If we train ourselves to think before we act in all ordinary affairs, then if an accident or anything else should happen in which prompt action is necessary, the swift mind will balance up the demands of the moment and direct swift action, but there will be no hurry, no inconsiderate, unwise blundering.

" But should I not follow my intuition? " some one may ask. Impulse and intuition are too often confused, though radically different in origin and characteristics. Impulse springs from the desire-nature, from the consciousness working through the astral body, and is an energy flung outwards in response to a stimulus from outside, an energy undirected by the intelligence, hasty, unconsidered, headlong. Intuition springs from the spiritual Ego, and is an energy flowing outwards to meet a demand from outside, an energy directed by the spiritual Ego, strong, calm, purposeful. For distinguishing between the two, until the nature is thoroughly balanced, calm consideration is necessary, and delay is essential; an impulse dies away under such consideration and delay; an intuition grows clearer and stronger under such conditions; calmness enables the lower mind to hear it and to feel its serene imperiousness. Moreover, if what seems to be an intuition is really a suggestion from some higher Being, that suggestion will sound the louder for our quiet meditation, and will lose nothing of force by such calm delay.

It is true that there is a certain pleasure in the abandonment to the headlong impulse, and that the imposed restraint is painful for a time. But the effort to lead the higher life is full of these renounceals of pleasure and acceptances of pain, and gradually we come to feel that there is a higher joy in the quiet considerate action than in the yielding to the tumultuous impulse, and that we have eliminated a constant source of regret. For constantly does such yielding prove a source of sorrow, and the impulse is found to be a mistake. If the proposed action be good, the purpose to perform it will be made stronger, not weaker, by careful thought. And if the purpose grows weaker with the thinking, then is it sure that it comes from the lower source, not from the higher.

Daily meditation, careful consideration before speech, the refusal to yield to impulse, these are the chief methods of turning the emotions into useful servants instead of dangerous masters.

4. THE USING OF EMOTION

Only he can use an emotion who has become its master and who knows that the emotions are not himself but are playing in the vehicles in which he dwells and are due to the interaction between the Self and the Not-Self. Their ever-changing nature marks them as belonging to the vehicles; they are stirred into activity by things without, answered to by the consciousness within. The attribute of consciousness that gives rise to emotions is Bliss, and pleasure and pain are the motions in the desire-vehicle caused by the contacts of the outer world, and by the response through it to these of the Self as Bliss; just as thoughts are the motions due to similar contacts and to the response to them of the Self as Knowledge. As the Self knows itself and distinguishes itself from its vehicles, it becomes ruler of the emotions, and pleasure and pain become equally modes of Bliss.

As progress is made, it will be found that greater equilibrium is attained under stress of pleasure and pain, and that the emotions no longer upset the balance of the mind. So long as pleasure elates and pain paralyzes, so that the performance of duty is hindered and hampered, so long is a man the slave, and not the ruler, of his emotions. When he has learned to rule them, the greatest wave of pleasure, the keenest sting of pain, can be felt, and yet the mind will remain steady and address itself calmly to the work in hand. Then whatever comes is turned into use. Out of pain is gained power, as out of pleasure are gained vitality and courage. All become forces to help instead of obstacles to hinder.

Of these uses oratory may serve as an illustration. You hear a man fired by passion, his words tumbling over each other, his gestures violent; he is possessed by, carried away by, emotion, but he does not sway his audience. The orator who sways is the master of his emotions and uses them to affect his audience; his words are deliberate and well chosen even in the rush of his speech, his gestures appropriate and dignified. He is not feeling the emotions, but *he has felt them*, and he now uses his past to shape the present. In proportion as a speaker has felt and has risen above his emotions will be his power to use them. No one without strong emotions can be a great speaker; but the greatness grows as the emotions are brought under control. A more effective explosion results from a careful arrangement of the explosive and a deliberate application of the match than by flinging them down anyhow, and the match after them, in the hope that something may catch.

So long as anyone is stirred by the emotions, the clear vision needed for helpful service is blurred. The valuable helper is the man who is calm and balanced while full of sympathy. What sort of a doctor would he be who in the midst of performing an operation should burst into tears? Yet many people are so distressed by the sight of suffering that their whole being is shaken by it, and they thus increase the suffering instead of relieving it. All emotion causes strong vibrations, and these pass from one to another. The effective helper must be calm and steady, remaining unshaken and radiating peace. One who stands on a rock above the waves can help another to gain that vantage-ground better than if he were himself battling with the waves.

Another use of the emotions when they are thoroughly in hand is to call up and use the appropriate one to rouse in another person an emotion beneficial to him. If a person be angry, the natural answer to his vibrations is anger in the one he meets, for all vibrations tend to be sympathetically reproduced. As we all have emotion-bodies, any body vibrating near us in a particular way tends to cause similar vibrations in us, if we have in our bodies the appropriate matter. Anger awakens anger, love awakens love, gentleness awakens gentleness. When we are masters of our emotions and feel the surge of anger rising in response to the vibrations of anger in another, we shall at once check this answer and shall let the waves of anger dash up against us, while we remain unmoved. The man who can hold his own emotion-body quiet, while those of others are vibrating strongly around him, has learned well the lesson of self-control. When this is done, he is ready to take the next step, to meet the vibration of an evil emotion with the vibration of the corresponding good emotion, and thus he not only witholds himself from anger, but sends out vibrations that tend to quiet the anger-vibrations of the other. He answers anger by love, wrath by gentleness.

At first, this answer must be deliberate, of set purpose, and angry people can be taken to practise

on. When one comes in our way, we utilize him.
The attempt will be, doubtless, cold and dry in the
beginning, with only the will to love in it and none
of the emotion; but after a while, the will to love
will produce a little emotion, and at last a habit
will be established, and kindness will be the spontaneous answer to unkindness. The steady, deliberate practice of answering thus the vibrations of
wrong emotions reaching us from outside will
establish a habit in the emotion-body, and it will
respond rightly automatically.

The teaching of all the great Masters of Ethics
is the same: "Return good for evil." And the
teaching is based on this interchange of vibrations
caused by love-and hate-emotions. The return of
evil intensifies it, while the return of good neutralizes
the evil. To stir love-emotions in others by sending
to them a stream of such emotions, so as to stimulate
all that is good in them and to weaken all that is
bad, is the highest use to which we can put our
emotions in daily human service. It is a good plan
to bear in mind a list of correspondences in emotions
and to practise accordingly, answering pride by
humility, discourtesy by compassion, arrogance by
submission, harshness by gentleness, irritability by
calmness. Thus is a nature built up which answers
all evil emotions by the corresponding good ones,
and which acts as a benediction on all around,

lessening the evil in them and strengthening the good.

5. THE VALUE OF EMOTION IN EVOLUTION

We have seen that emotion is the motive power in man, and to turn it into a helper in evolution we must utilize it to lift and not allow it to degrade. The Ego, in his evolution, needs " points to draw him " upwards, as says *The Voice of the Silence*, for the upward way is steep, and an attractice object above us, towards which we can strive, is an aid impossible to overestimate. Only too often we lag on the way, and feel no desire to proceed; aspiration is inert, the longing to rise has fled. Then may we summon emotion to our aid, by twining it around some object of devotion, and thus gain the impetus we need, the lifting force we crave.

This form of emotion is what is often called hero-worship, the power to admire and love greatly one who is nobler than oneself; and to be able thus to love and admire is to have at disposal one of the great lifting forces in human evolution. Hero-worship is often decried because a perfect ideal is not possible to find among men living in the world, but a partial ideal that can be loved and emulated is a help in quickening evolution. It is true that there will be weakenesses in such a partial ideal, and it is

necessary to distinguish between the heroic qualities
and the weaknesses found in conjunction with
them; but the attention should be fixed on the heroic
qualities that stimulate, and not on the blemishes
that mar every one who has not as yet transcended
humanity. To recognize that the weaknesses are of
the Not-Self and are passing, while the nobility is
of the Self that endures, to love what is great and
to be able to pass over what is small, that is the
spirit that leads to discipleship of the Great Ones.
Only good is gained by the hero-worshipper from
his ideal, if he honour the greatness and disregard
the weakness, and on the hero himself will fall the
karma of his own shortcomings.

But it is said: if we thus recognize the nobility
of the Self in the midst of human weaknesses, we
are only doing what we should do with all, and why
make a hero out of anyone in whom there is still any
human weakness? Because of the help our hero
gives us as an inspiration and a measure of our own
achievement. No ordinary person can be turned
into a hero; it is only when the Self shines out with
more than ordinary lustre that the inclination to
hero-worship arises. The man *is* a hero, though
not yet superhuman, and his weaknesses are but as
spots in the sun. There is a proverb which says:
"No man is a hero to his valet-de-chambre," and
the cynic reads this as meaning that the most heroic

man owes his greatness to distance. But is not the meaning rather that the valet-soul, intent on the shine of a boot and the set of a necktie, cannot appreciate that which makes the hero, having naught in him that can sound sympathetically with the notes the hero strikes? For to be able to admire means to be able to achieve, and love and reverence for the great is a sign that a man is growing like them.

When emotion is thus aroused, we should judge ourselves by our ideal, and be ashamed to do or think aught that would bring a shade of sorrow over the eyes of him we revere. His presence should be with us as an uplifter, until, judging ourselves in the light of the greater achievement, we find ourselves also beginning to achieve.

That the pure light of the Self shines through none who walk the miry paths of earth is true, but there are some through whom enough light shines to lighten the darkness, and to help us to see where to plant our feet. It is better to thank and honour these, to rejoice and be glad in them, than to belittle them because they are not wholly of heaven, because some touches of human weakness still entangle their feet. Blessed indeed are they who have in themselves the hero-nature and hence recognize their elder kin; for them waits the open gate to the upper reaches, and the more they love, the more they honour, the swifter will be their approach to that gateway. No better karma comes to a man than to find the hero who may bear him company to the entering; no sadder karma than to have seen him, in an illuminated moment, and then to have cast him aside, blinded by an imperfection he is outgrowing.

CHAPTER VI

THE WILL

1. THE WILL WINNING ITS FREEDOM

WE return now to the consideration of that power in man with which we started—the Will. The student will remember that it was stated that it was the Will of the Self, of the individualized Self—individualized though as yet unconscious of its individualization—which drew him into manifestation. Not by compulsion, not by external necessity, not by anything opposed to him from outside, but by the great Will of which his own Will is part—his Will individualized as a centre but not yet cut off by circumference of matter—pulsing in him as the life-blood of the mother pulses in the yet unborn child, he reaches forth towards manifestation, dimly longing for the rich thrill of life enveiled in matter, for the exercise of powers yearning for activity, for the experience of worlds tumultuously full of movement. That which consciously the Logos wills—the Logos willing to become incarnate in a universe—all the centres of individualized life within Him also will, though as it were blindly and groping towards a fuller life. It is the Will to live, to know, and that forthgoing Will sets to manifestation.

We have seen that this Will, the Power of the Self, becomes what we call Desire on the denser planes of matter, and that, blinded by matter and unable to see its way, its direction is determined by the attractions and repulsions playing upon it from external objects. Hence we cannot say of the Self at this period that he is Self-directed; he is directed by attractions and repulsions that touch him at this periphery. We have further seen that as Desire came into touch with Intelligence, and these two aspects of the Self played upon each other, emotions evolved, showing traces of their parentage, of their Desire-mother and of their Intelligence-father. And we have studied the methods by which emotion may be controlled, put to its true uses, and thus rendered serviceable instead of dangerous in human evolution.

We have now to consider how this Will, the hidden Power which has ever moved to activity though not yet controlling activity, slowly wins to freedom, that is, to Self-determination. In a moment we shall consider what is meant by this word " freedom ".

Essentially and fundamentally free in its origin as the Power of the Self, Will has become bound and limited in its attempts to master the matter into which the Self has entered. We need not shrink from saying that matter masters the Self, not the Self matter, and this it does by virtue of the Self regarding matter as himself, identifying himself with it; as he wills through it, thinks through it, acts through it, it becomes to him verily himself, and deluded he cries: " I am this! " and while it limits him and binds him, he, feeling it to be himself, cries: " I am free." Yet is this mastering of the Self by matter but a temporary thing, for the matter is ever changing, coming and going, impermanent, and is ever being shaped and unconsciously drawn round and rejected by the unfolding forces of the Self, permanent amid the impermanent.

Let us come to the stage in human evolution in which memory has grown stronger than the instinctive outgoing to the pleasant and withdrawing from the painful; in which Intelligence rules Desires, and reason has triumphed over impulse. The result of the age-long evolution is to be reaped, and part of that result is freedom.

While the Will is expressing itself as Desire, determined in its direction by outside attractions, it it obviously not free, but very distinctly bound. Just as any living creature might be dragged by a force greater than its own force in a direction unchosen by it, so is the Will dragged away by the attraction of objects, pulled along the path which promises pleasure, which is agreeable to pursue; it is not active as a Self-determined force, but on the contrary the Self is being dragged away by an external and compelling attraction.

No more vivid picture of the Self, under these conditions, can be given than that before quoted from an ancient Hindu Scripture, in which the Self is limned as the rider in a chariot, and the senses, attracted by pleasure-giving objects, are the ungovernable horses that carry away the chariot of the body and the helpless rider within it. Although the Will be the very Power of the Self, so long as the Self is being carried away by these unruly horses, he is emphatically bound and not free. It is idle to speak of a free Will in a man who is the slave of the objects around him. He is ever in bondage, he can exercise no choice; for though we may think of such a one as choosing to follow the path along which attractions draw him, there is in truth no choice nor thought of choice. So long as attractions and repulsions determine the path, all talk of freedom is empty and foolish. Even though a man feels himself as choosing the desirable object, the feeling of freedom is illusory, for he is dragged by the attractiveness of the object and the longing for pleasure in himself. He is as much, or as little, free as the iron is free to move to the magnet. The

21

movement is determined by the strength of the magnet and the nature of the iron answering to its attraction.

To understand what we mean by freedom of the Will, we must clear away a preliminary difficulty which faces us in the word " choice ". When we appear to be free to choose, does that so-called freedom of choice mean freedom of Will? Or is it not true to say that freedom of choice only means that no external force compels us to elect one or another of alternatives? But the important question that lies behind this is: " What makes us choose? " Whether we are free to act when we have chosen is a very different thing from whether we are " free " to choose, or whether the choice is determined by something that lies behind.

How often we hear it said as a proof of the freedom of the Will: " I am free to choose whether I will leave the room or not; I am free to choose whether I will drop this weight or not." But such argument is beside the question. No one denies the power of a person, physically unconstrained, to leave a room or to stay in it, to drop a weight or to uphold it. The interesting question is: " Why do I choose? " When we analyse the choice, we see that it is determined by motive, and the determinist argues: " Your muscles can uphold or drop the weight, but if there is a valuable and fragile article underneath, you will not choose to drop it. That which determines your choice not to drop it is the presence of that fragile object. Your choice is determined by motives, and the strongest motive directs it." The question is not: "Am I free to act?" but: "Am I free to will?" And we see clearly that the Will is determined by the strongest motive, and that, so far as that goes, the determinist is right.

In truth, this fact that the Will is determined by the strongest motive is the basis of all organized society, of all law, of all penalty, of all responsibility, of all education. The man whose will is not thus determined is irresponsible, insane. He is a creature who cannot be appealed to, cannot be reasoned with, cannot be relied on, a person without reason, logic, or memory, without the attributes we regard as human. In law, a man is regarded as irresponsible when no motive sways him, when no ordinary reasons affect him; he is insane, and is not amenable to legal penalties. A Will which is an energy pointing in any direction, pushing to action without motive, without reason, without sense, might perhaps be called " free", but this is not what is meant by " freedom of the Will ". That Will is determined by the strongest motive must be taken for granted in any sane discussion of the freedom of the Will.

What then is meant by the freedom of the Will? It can be but a conditioned, a relative, freedom at most, for the separated Self is a part of a whole, and the whole must be greater than, must compel, all its parts. And this is true alike of the Self and of the bodies in which he is ensheathed. None questions that the bodies are in a realm of law and move within law, can move but by the law, and the freedom with which they move is but in relation to each other and by virtue of the interplay of the countless forces which balance each other variously and endlessly, and in this variety and endlessness offer innumerable possibilities and thus a freedom of movement within a rigidity of bondage. And the Self also is in a realm of law, nay is himself the very law, as being part of that nature which is the Being of all beings. No separated Self may escape from the Self which is all, and, however freely he may move with regard to other separated Selves, he may not, cannot, move outside the life which informs him, which is his nature and his law, in which he lives and moves. The parts constrain not the parts, the separated Selves constrain not the separated Selves; but the whole constrains and controls the parts, the Self constrains and controls the Selves. Yet even here, since the Selves are the Self, freedom starts up from amid apparent bondage, and " none else compels ".

This freedom of a part as regards other parts while in bondage to the whole may be seen clearly in physical nature. We are parts of a world whirling through space and revolving also on its own axis, turning eastwards ever. Of this we know naught, since its motion carries us with it, and all moves together and at once, and in one direction. Eastwards we turn with our world, and naught we can do will change our direction. Yet with regard to each other and to the places about us, we can move freely and change our relative positions. I may go to the west of a person or a place, though we are both whirling eastwards ceaselessly. And of the motion of a part with regard to a part I shall be conscious, small and slow as it is, while of the vast swift whirling that carries all parts eastwards and onwards ever, I shall be utterly unconscious, and shall say in my ignorance: "Behold, I have moved westwards." And the high Gods might laugh contemptuously at the ignorance of the fragment that speaks of the direction of its motion, were it not that They, being wise, know of the movements within the motion, and of the truth which is false and yet true.

And yet again may we see how the great Will works onwards undeviatingly along the path of evolution, and compels all to travel along that path, and still leaves to each to choose his method of going, and the fashion of his unconscious working. For the carrying out of that Will needs every fashion of working and every method of going, and takes up and utilizes all. A man shapes himself to a noble character, and nourishes lofty aspirations, and seeks ever to do loyal and faithful service to his fellows; then shall he be brought to birth where great opportunities cry aloud for workers, and the Will shall be wrought out by him in a nation that needs such helping, and he shall fill a hero's part. The part is written by the great Author; the ability to fill it is of the man's own making. Or a man yields to every temptation and becomes apt to evil, and he uses ill such power as he has, and disregards mercy, justice, and truth in petty ways and in daily life; then shall he be brought to birth where oppression is needed, and cruelty, and ill ways, and the Will shall be wrought out by him also in a nation that is working out the results of an evil past, and he shall be of the weaklings that tyrannize cruelly and meanly and shame the nation that bears them. Again is the part written by the great Author, and the ability to fill it is of the man's own making. So work the little Wills within the great Will.

Seeing, then, that the Will is determined by motive conditioned by the limits of the matter that enveils the separated Self, and by the Self whereof the Self exercising the Will is part—what mean we by the freedom of the Will? We mean, surely, that freedom is to be determined from within, bondage is to be determined from without; the Will is free, when the Self, willing to act, draws his motive for that volition from sources that lie within himself, and has not the motive acting upon him from sources outside.

And truly this is freedom, for the greater Self in which he moves is one with him: " I am That "; and the vaster Self in which moves that greater Self is one with that vaster, and says also: " I am That "; and so on and on, in huger and huger sweeps, if world-systems and universe-systems be thought of; yet may the lowliest " I " that knows himself turn inwards and not outwards, and know himself as one with the Inner Self, the Pratyagatma, the one, and therefore truly free. Looking outwards he is ever bound, though the limits of his bondage recede endlessly, unlimitedly; looking inwards he is ever free, for he is Brahman, the Eternal.

When a man is Self-determined, then we may say that the man is free in every sense in which the word freedom is valuable, and his Self-determination is not bondage, in any harassing sense of that word. That which in my innermost Self I will to do, that to which none other forces me, that bears the mark which distinguishes between the free and the bound. How far in us, in this sense of the word freedom, can we say that our Will is free? For the most part, but few of us can claim this freedom in any more than a small portion. Apart from the previously-mentioned bondage to attractions and repulsions, we are bound within the channels made by our past thinkings, by our habits—most of all by our habits of thought—by the qualities and the absence of qualities brought over from past lives, by the strength and the weaknesses that were born with us, by our education and our surroundings, by the imperious compulsions of our stage in evolution, our physical heredity, and our national and racial traditions. Hence only a narrow path is left to us in which our Will can run; it strikes itself ever against the past, which appears as walls in the present.

To all intents and purposes the Will of us is not free. It is only in process of becoming free, and it will only be free when the Self has utterly mastered his vehicles and uses them for his own purposes, when every vehicle is only a vehicle, completely responsive to his every impulse, and not a struggling animal, ill-broken, with desires of its own.[1] When the Self has transcended ignorance, vanquishing the habits that are the marks of past ignorance, then is the Self free, and then will be realized the meaning

[1] This is only accomplished when the life of the Self informs the matter of his vehicles, instead of the downward-striving elemental essence, i.e., when the law of the Spirit of Life replaces the law of sin and death.

of the paradox, " in whose service is perfect freedom ". For then will it be realized that separation
is not, that the separated Will is not, that, by virtue
of our inherent Divinity, our Will is part of the
Divine Will, and that it is which has given us
throughout our long evolution the strength to carry
on that evolution, and that the realization of the
unity of Will is the realization of freedom.

Along these lines of thought it is that some have
found the ending of the age-long controversy between the " freedom " of the Will and determinism,
and, while recognizing the truth battled for by
determinism, have also preserved and justified the
inherent feeling: " I am free, I am not bound."
That idea of spontaneous energy, of forthgoing
power from the inner recesses of our being, is based
on the very essence of consciousness, on the " I "
which is the Self, that Self which, because divine,
is free.

2. WHY SO MUCH STRUGGLE?

As we survey the long course of evolution, the
slow process of the development of the Will, the
question inevitably rises in the mind: " Why should
there be all this struggle and difficulty? Why should
there be so many mistakes and so many falls? Why
this long bondage before freedom can be attained? "

Before replying to this, a general position must be laid down. In answering any question, the limits of that question must be borne in mind, and the answer must not be judged to be inadequate because it does not answer another question that is all the time present in the background. An answer to a question may be adequate without being a final answer to all questions; and its adequacy is not rightly gauged if it be thrown aside as not answering a further question which may be propounded. Half the dissatisfaction of many students arises from a restless impatience that will not deal in any kind of order with the questions that come thronging to the mind, but demands that they should all be answered at once, and that the answer to one question should cover all the others. The adequacy of means must be judged in relation to the end which those means are designed to bring about. In all cases the answer must be judged by its relevancy to the question asked, and not by its not replying to some other allied question lying at the back of the mind. Thus, the relevancy of any means found to exist in a universe must be decided by an end found to be aimed at in that universe, and they must not be judged as though offered as an answer to the further question: " Why should there be any universe at all? " That question may indeed be asked and answered, but the proof of the adequacy of a means in a universe to an end, seen to be aimed at in that universe, will not be that answer. And it is no evidence that the answer to the original question is inadequate, if the questioner replies: " Yes but why should there be a universe? " In replying to the question: " Why should there be all these mistakes and falls in treading the path of evolution? " we must take the universe as existing, as a fact to start with, and must study it in order to discover the end, or, at least, one of the ends, towards which it is tending. Why it should tend thitherward is, as said, a further question, and one of profoundest interest; but it is by the discovered end that we must judge the means employed to reach it.

Even a cursory study of the part of the universe in which we find ourselves shows us that one at least of its ends—if not its end—is to produce living beings of high intelligence and strong will, capable of taking an active part in carrying on and guiding the activities of Nature and of co-operating in the general scheme of evolution. Further study, carried on by the unfolding of the inner qualities and endorsed by ancient writings, shows us that this world is not alone, but forms one of a series, that it has been aided in the evolution of its humanity by men of elder growth, and is to yield men of its own growing for the aiding of younger worlds in ages yet unborn. Moreover, it shows also a vast hierarchy of superhuman Beings, directing and guiding evolution, and as the centre of the universe the threefold Logos, Ruler and Lord of His system; and it tells that the fruitage of a system is not only a great hierarchy of mighty Intelligences, with ranks of ever-lessening splendour stretching below them, but also this supreme perfection of a Logos as the crown of all. And it unveils vista after vista of increasing splendour, universes where each system is but as a world and so on and on, in ever-widening range of illimitable glorious fullness of life unending. And then the question rises: "By what means shall be evolved these mighty Ones, who climb from the dust to the stars, and from those stars that are the dust of vaster systems to the stars that are to them as our mire to our sun?"

Thus studied, imagination fails to find a path by which these self-poised, self-determined Beings can reach that perfect equilibrium and steadfast inerrancy of wisdom that fits them to be the "nature" of a system, save just that path of struggle and of experience along which we strive to-day. For could there be an extra-cosmic God with nature other than that of the Self we see unfolding around us in harmonious certainty of linked sequence, with nature irregular and fitful, changing and arbitrary, incalculable, then it might be that out of that chaos might be flung up a being called "perfect", but truly most imperfect, since most limited, who, having no experience behind him, and therefore without reason and without judgment, might as a machine act "rightly" in, *i.e.*, in accordance with, any given scheme of things, and grind out as does a machine, the sequence of movements arranged for it. But such a being would only fit his scheme, and outside it would be useless, incompetent. Nor would there here be life, which is the changing self-adaptation to changing conditions, without the loss, the disintegration of its centre. By the troublous path along which we are climbing, we are being prepared for all emergencies in the universe in the future with which we may have to do, and that is a result well worth the trials to which we are exposed.

Nor must we forget that we are here because we have willed to unfold our powers through the experiences of life on the lower planes; that our lot is self-chosen, not imposed; that we are in the world as the result of our own "Will to Live"; that if that Will changed—though truly it is not so changeful—we should cease to live here and return to the Peace, without gathering the harvest for which we came. "None else compels."

3. THE POWER OF THE WILL

This power—which has ever been recognized in Occultism as the spiritual energy in man, one in kind with that which sends forth, supports, and calls in the worlds—is now being groped after in the outer world, and is being almost unconsciously used by many as a means of bringing about results otherwise unattainable. The schools of Christian Science, Mental Science, Mind-Cure, etc., are all dependent for their results on the outflowing power of the Will. Diseases yield to that flow of energy, and not only nervous disorders as some imagine. Nervous disorders yield the most readily, because the nervous system has been shaped for the expression of spiritual powers on the physical plane. The results are the most rapid where the sympathetic system is first worked upon, for that is the more directly related to the aspect of Will, in the form of Desire, as the cerebro-spinal is more directly related to the aspects of Cognition and of pure Will. The dispersion of tumours, cancers, etc., and the destruction of their causes, the curing of lesions and bone-fractures, imply for the most part considerable knowledge on the part of the healer. I say "for the most part", because it is possible that the Will may be guided from the higher plane even where physical plane knowledge is lacking, in the case of an operator at an advanced stage of evolution. The method of cure, where knowledge is present, would be as follows. The operator would form a mental picture of the affected organ in a state of perfect health, creating that part in mental stuff by the imagination; he would then build into it astral matter, thus densifying the image, and would then use the force of magnetism to densify it further by etheric matter, building the denser materials of gases, liquids, and solids into this mould, utilizing the materials available in the body and supplying from outside any deficiencies. In all this the Will is the guiding energy, and such manipulation of matter is merely a question of knowledge, whether on this or on the higher planes. There is not the danger in cures wrought by this method that accompanies those wrought by an easier, and therefore commoner, system, by the working on the sympathetic system alluded to above.

People are advised, in some of the methods now popularized, to concentrate their thoughts on the solar plexus, and to " live under its control ". The sympathetic system governs the vital processes—the functioning of the heart, lungs, digestive apparatus —and the solar plexus forms its most important centre. Now the carrying on of these vital processes has, as before explained,[1] passed under the

[1] See Part I, Chapter X, § 1.

control of the sympathetic system in the course of evolutions, as the cerebro-spinal system has become more and more dominant. And the reviving of the control of this system by the Will, by a process of concentration of thought, is a retrograde and not a forward step, even though it often brings about a certain degree of clairvoyance. This method, as already said, is much followed in India in the system called Hatha Yoga, and the student learns to control the action of the heart, lungs, and digestive apparatus; he can thus inhibit the beating of the heart, can stop the lungs, can reverse peristaltic action, and so on. And when it is done, the question arises: What have you gained by your success? You have brought again under the control of the Will a system which in course of evolution had been rendered automatic, to the great convenience of the owner of these lower functions; and have thus taken a step backward in evolution. To do this means failure in the long run, even though there may be for the moment a palpable result to show.

Moreover, the concentration of thought on a centre of the sympathetic system and, most of all, on the solar plexus, means a serious physical danger, unless the learner be under the physical observation of his teacher, or be able to receive and bring through to the physical brain the instructions that may be given to him on a higher plane. Concentration on the solar plexus is apt to bring on disease of a peculiarly intractable kind. It issues in a profound melancholy almost impossible to remove, in fits of terrible depression, and sometimes in a form of paralysis. Not along these lines should travel the serious student, intent on the knowledge of the Self. When that knowledge is obtained, the body becomes the instrument on which the Self can play, and all that is needed meanwhile is to purify and refine it, so that it may come into harmony with the higher bodies and be prepared to vibrate rhythmically with them. The brain will thus be rendered more responsive, and by industrious thinking and the action of meditation— not on the brain, but on lofty ideas—it will be gradually improved. The brain becomes a better organ as it is exercised, and this is on the road of evolution. But to work directly on the sympathetic plexuses is on the road of retrogression. Many a one comes, asking for deliverance from the results of these practices, and one can only sadly answer: " To undo the mischief will take years." Results may be gained quickly by going backwards, but it is better to face the upward climbing, and then utilize the physical instrument from above, not from below.

There is another matter to be considered in healing diseases by Will—the danger of driving the

22

disease into a higher vehicle, in driving it out of the physical body. Disease is often the final working out of the evil that existed previously on the higher planes, and it is then far better to let it thus work out than to forcibly check it and throw it back into the subtler vehicle. It is the last working out of an evil desire or an evil thought, and in such a case the use of physical means of cure is safer than the use of mental means, for the former cannot cast it back into the higher planes, whereas the latter may do so. Curative mesmerism does not run this danger, belonging as it does to the physical plane; that may be used by any one whose life, thoughts, and desires are pure. But the moment Will forces are poured down into the physical, there is a danger of reaction, and of the driving of the disease back into the subtler vehicles from which it came forth.

If mental curing is done by the purification of thought and desire, and the natural quiet working of the purified thoughts and desires on the physical body, no harm can result; to restore physical harmony by making harmonious the mental and astral vehicles is a true method of mental healing, but it is not as rapid as the Will-cure and is far harder. Purity of mind means health of body and it is this idea—that where the mind is pure the body should be healthy—that has led many to adopt these mental methods of healing.

A person whose mind is perfectly pure and balanced will not generate fresh bodily disease, though he may have some unexhausted karma to work off, or he may take on himself some of the disharmonies caused by others. Purity and health truly go together. When, as is and has been the case, some saint is found to be suffering physically, then such a one is either working out the effect of bad thinking in the past, or is bearing in himself something of the world's disharmony, turning on to himself the forces of disharmony, harmonizing them within his own vehicles and sending them forth again as currents of peace and goodwill. Many have been puzzled by seeing that the greatest and the purest suffer, both mentally and physically. They suffer for others, not for themselves, and they are truly White Magicians, transmuting by spiritual alchemy, in the crucible of their own suffering bodies, the base metals of human passions into the pure gold of love and peace.

Apart from the question of the ways of working on the body by the Will, another question arises in the thoughtful mind: Is it well to use the Will in this fashion for our own helping? Is there not a certain degradation in using the highest power of the Divine within us in the service of our body, to bring about merely a good condition of physical health? Is it well that the Divine should thus turn stones into bread, and so fall under the very temptation resisted by the Christ? The story may be taken historically or mythically, it matters not; it contains a profound spiritual truth and an instance of obedience to an occult law. Still remains true the answer of the tempted: " Man does not live by bread alone, but by every word that proceedeth out of the mouth of God." This ethic seems to be on a higher plane than that which yokes the Divine to the service of the physical body. One of the dangers of the present is the worship of the body, the putting of the body on too high a pinnacle—a reaction from exaggerated asceticism. By using the Will to serve the body, we make the Will its slave, and the practice of continually removing little aches and pains by willing them to go saps the higher quality of endurance. A person thus acting is apt to be irritable under small physical discomforts which the Will cannot remove, and the higher power of the Will which can control the body and support it in its work, even though it be suffering, is undermined. Hesitance to use the power of the Will for relief of one's body need not arise from any doubt as to the soundness of the thought, the reality of the law, on which such action is based; but from a fear that men may fall under the temptation of using that which should lift them to realms spiritual as the minister of the physical, and may thus become slaves of the body, and be helpless when the body fails them in the hour of need.

It is an occult law, binding on every Initiate, that he may not use an occult power for his own helping; if he do, he loses the power to help others, and it is not worth while to forfeit the great for the small. That already-referred-to story of the temptation of the Christ has a further-reaching significance than most understand. Had He used His occult power to turn stones into bread for the relief of His hunger, instead of waiting in patient strength for the food brought by the Shining Ones, He would not later have been able to endure the mystic sacrifice of the Cross. The taunt then flung at Him contained an occult truth: " He saved others: Himself He cannot save." He could not use, to spare Himself one pang, the powers that had opened the eyes of the blind and made the leper clean. Those who would save themselves must give up the divine mission of being Saviours of the world. They must choose between the one and the other as they evolve. If in their evolution they choose the lower, and use the great powers they have won for the service of themselves and of the body, then must they give up the higher mission of using them for the redemption of the race. There is such an immense activity of mind at the present time that the need is all the greater for the employment of its powers to the highest ends.

4. WHITE AND BLACK MAGIC

Magic is the use of the Will to guide the powers of external nature, and is truly, as its name implies, the great science. The human Will, being the power of the Divine in man, can subjugate and control the inferior energies, and thus bring about the results desired. The difference between White and Black Magic lies in the motive which determines the Will; when that Will is set to benefit others, to help and bless all who come within its scope, then is the man a White Magician, and the results which he brings about by the exercise of his trained Will are beneficial, and aid the course of human evolution. He is ever expanding by such exercise, becoming less and less separate from his kind, and is a centre of far-reaching help. But when the Will is exercised for the advantage of the lower self, when it is employed for personal ends and aims, then is the man a Black Magician, a danger to the race, and his results obstruct and delay human evolution. He is ever contracting by such exercise, becoming more and more separate from his kind, shutting himself within a shell which isolates him, and which grows ever thicker and denser with the exercise of his trained powers. The Will of the Magician is ever strong, but the Will of the White Magician is strong with the strength of life, flexible at need, rigid at need, ever assimilating to the great Will, the Law of the universe. The Will of the Black Magician has the strength of iron, pointing ever to the personal end, and it strikes against the great Will, and sooner or later must shiver itself into pieces against it. It is the peril of Black Magic against which the student of occultism is guarded by the law which forbids him to use his occult powers for himself; for though no man is a Black Magician who does not deliberately erect his personal Will against the great Law, it is well to recognize the essence of Black Magic and to check the very beginnings of evil. Just as it was said above that the saint harmonizing the forces of disharmony within himself is truly the White Magician, so is he the Black Magician who uses for his own gain all the forces he has acquired by knowledge, turns them to the service of his own separateness, and increases the disharmony of the world by his selfish graspings, while seeking to preserve harmony in his own vehicles.

5. ENTERING INTO PEACE

When the Self has grown so indifferent to the vehicles in which he dwells that their vibrations can no longer affect him; when he can use them for any purpose; when his vision has become perfectly clear;

when the vehicles offer no opposition, since the elemental life has left them, and only the life flowing from himself animates them; then the Peace enfolds him and the object of the long struggle is attained. Such a one, Self-centred, no longer confuses himself with his vehicles. They are instruments to work with, tools to manipulate at his will. He has then realized the peace of the Master, the one who is utterly master of his vehicles, and therefore master of life and death. Capable of receiving into them the tumult of the world and of reducing it to harmony; capable of feeling through them the sufferings of others, but not sufferings of his own; he stands apart from, beyond, all storms. Yet is he able ever to bend down into the storm to lift another above it, without losing his own foothold on the rock of the Divine, consciously recognized as himself. Such are truly Masters, and Their peace may now and then be felt, for a time at least, by those who are striving to tread the same path, who have not yet reached that same rock of the Self-conscious Divine.

That union of the separate Will with the one Will for the helping of the world is the goal which seems to be more worthy of reaching after than aught the world can offer. Not to be separate from men, but one with them; not to win peace and bliss alone, but to say with the Chinese Blessed One: " Never will I enter into final peace alone;

but always and everywhere will I suffer and strive until all enter with me "—that is the crown of humanity. In proportion as we can realize that the suffering and the striving are the more efficacious as we suffer only in the sufferings of others and feel not suffering for ourselves, we shall rise into the Divine, shall tread the " razor path " that the Great Ones have trodden, and shall find that the Will, which has guided us along that path, and which has realized itself in the treading of that path, is strong enough still to suffer and to strive, until the suffering and the strife for all are over, and all together enter into Peace.

PEACE TO ALL BEINGS

INDEX

PAGE

23